THE MAKING OF A
WARRIOR OF LIGHT

CONQUERING PAIN TO CLAIM YOUR POWER

A MEMOIR

Theresa Rubi Garcia

GARCIA, THERESA, Author
THE MAKING OF A WARRIOR OF LIGHT
THERESA GARCIA

Published by
ELITE ONLINE PUBLISHING
63 East 11400 South #230
Sandy, UT 84070
EliteOnlinePublishing.com

Edited by: Karen Que

ISBN: 978-1-956642-93-3 (Paperback)
ISBN: 978-1-956642-94-0 (Hardback)
ISBN: 978-1-961801-47-9 (Audiobook)
ISBN: 978-1-956642-95-7 (eBook)

Library of Congress Control Number: 2025910619

BIO038000
BIO022000

QUANTITY PURCHASES: Schools, companies, professional groups, clubs, and other organizations may qualify for special terms when ordering quantities of this title. For information, email theresa@rpempowerment.com

PRAISES

"This is a page-turner! Even though parts of it may be difficult to read. Garcia really delves into the mindset she was in at every step of this journey through her life, showing with raw honesty how she survived, moved forward, and learned to overcome the adversities of both nurture and nature. This story could have been a tragedy, and many parts are indeed tragic, but Garcia's hope and indomitable spirit shine through. Truly a warrior in life, and a light in this world."

—Celeste Johnson

"The Making of a Warrior of Light is more than just a memoir; it's a masterclass in healing, resilience, and reclaiming one's power. Theresa's life story is raw, unfiltered, and utterly courageous. From a childhood marked by unthinkable abuse, poverty, racism, and neglect to becoming a loving mother, community leader, and spiritual guide, her journey is nothing short of extraordinary."

—James Hilliard

"Theresa's story is a miracle in motion. She kept it all the way real, sharing pain that most people stay silent about. As a beta reader, I saw the rawness, the resilience, and the light breaking through. This memoir isn't just survival, it's a sacred testimony. Theresa is a true warrior, and her story lights the way for others still fighting their way through."

—Angela July

DEDICATION

This book unfolds as a tribute to the luminaries in my life, whose light has guided me through the shadows and into the brilliance of self-realization. At the heart of this odyssey is Mauriion Lavell Price, my son and beacon of love. His arrival marked the dawn of an unparalleled love, a transformative force that reshaped my very essence, step by patient step. Mauriion, you are the architect of my purpose, the genesis of a love so profound it has become my compass.

To my beloved nieces and nephews, this dedication also embraces you. Each of you, unique in spirit and bound to me not just by blood but by an enduring affection, know that neither time's passage nor the vastness of space can dim the warmth I hold for you. In this journey of gratitude and recognition, I cannot overlook Katherine Harvickson, a visionary and founder of Quantum Ascension, whose faith in me was the lighthouse in my darkest storms. Katherine, with a heart as vast as the universe, extended her hand to me with nothing but pure intent, asking for nothing in return. Her belief, her unparalleled support during my lowest ebbs, and her unwavering conviction in my potential were the wings on which I soared to realms I once thought unattainable. Her mentorship, imbued with humanity and humility, was a catalyst for not only a thriving business but a rekindled hope in the goodness that humanity is capable of. Katherine, you are the embodiment of grace and the epitome of a true ally, whose actions ripple through the fabric of lives, uplifting and empowering.

This book, therefore, is more than a narrative; it is a clarion call to each reader to embody the essence of lifting others as we ascend. It is a testament to the transformative power of love, support, and belief in ourselves and one another. Let us tread this path together, for in the act of uplifting others, we discover the zenith of our own potential.

Visit https://rpempowerment.com/warrior-of-light
for updates and resources.

TABLE OF CONTENTS

PREFACE

I went from being a stripper to the Chief Empowerment Officer at Rubi's Positive Empowerment. A girl that grew up with so much trauma and self-hatred built a social impact company that has transformed the lives of hundreds of people through helping them reach and exceed business and career goals. I played a role in connecting businesses to over $1 billion in revenue all the while living in survival mode from my childhood. Now, I live my life day by day no longer defining who I am by what I do.

I had a lot of shame as a stripper and received a lot of judgment when, well, *if* I told others. Now, as soon as people hear what I do, I feel their instant respect. I find it funny, as soon as I don't need something—whatever it may be, it is there.

Like most people, I have been through so much in life. The difference between myself and others is that I chose to believe there was more to life than what my current reality presented to me, despite having no evidence for this belief. However, that belief saved me over and over again.

Just like Jesus, I truly believe we are all born with incredible gifts that simply need to be realized. The most precious of them all is that God made us and therefore is *in* us. I am God. You are God. When you realize that God is in the Earth, moon, stars, ocean and all that is, you will naturally honor, respect, value, and love yourself and all that is.

Does your heart palpitate at the idea that you are God? The Persian Poet Rumi says, "You are not a drop in the ocean, you are the entire ocean in a drop." What an audacious thought, will you contemplate being divinely audacious with me? Does this concept feel like a heavy burden and lot of responsibility? Or will you choose to see this as the most incredible adventure of allowing divine presence to come through your body, your vessel and carry out the will you are destined for? You deserve health, wealth, joy, and peace. Abundance is natural when you choose to embody your divine presence. Life happens, we get hurt, people pass away. Pain is inevitable, suffering is a choice. It is a choice to allow pain, fear, and three-dimensional evidence to shape your beliefs that end up limiting you.

I am here to show you that no matter what you go through, you have a choice to either see it as an opportunity for growth or to allow it to devastate or cripple you.

As someone who has been abused, neglected, rejected for the color of my skin, diagnosed with multiple disabilities, and grown-up poor without any role models or people who showed me true love, I could have allowed all of these things to cripple me. At times, they did. I have been an addict most of my life. I was a stripper with multiple sugar daddies. I was a teenage mom with no support from family. I was suicidal and depressed and at the lowest end of anyone's expectations for success. I believed I was ugly and stupid and unworthy of anything good. Yet, I overcame all of that.

The abuse and chaos I suffered as a child taught me that life is hard, so I figured I had to be harder in order to survive.

The tougher I became, the more hard stuff life threw at me to help me prove my warped definition of who I thought I was: a badass with no regard for what others thought of me; a hustler with a steel exterior but a heart of gold; a mother who would literally kill for her child; and a girl with hopes and dreams I was afraid to voice, but eventually achieved in spite of the odds against me.

Despite being a single mom at the tender age of fifteen and working as a stripper by the time I was eighteen, I chose to believe there was more to life than what my reality presented to me at that time. All of the abuse I encountered, and all of the choices I made, turned me into a Warrior of Light. As I share the horrors and successes of my life, I hope you reflect on yours and choose to honor all that has shaped you into the warrior you are today.

INTRODUCTION

My life is a perfect case story to illustrate that no matter what you go through, you have a choice of how to see it. You can view your circumstances as an opportunity for growth or you can allow every horrendous thing that happens to devastate or cripple you. No matter what hell I was going through, I somehow managed to see the former. This didn't happen all at once. I cried, became a victim, and then often had no choice but to move forward. By reflecting on my past, I was able to find the gifts that were right in front of my face, yet I was unable to see.

The journey I am going to take you on in this book will include a lot of pain. I want you to feel the emotions, release them, and commit to not feeling sorry for me. This book isn't to fuel pity. Rather, it is intended to be a roadmap for how to turn pain into power. I share the details so you can see that it doesn't matter where you come from or who is by your side. All that matters is your willingness to consciously choose a better life and to take the tiny action steps towards what you love and self-mastery, versus focusing on and perpetuating what you dislike.

I encourage you to read this book with an open heart and mind. If you feel triggered by anything you read, please write it down and then ask yourself, "Why did this statement or situation trigger me? What could be the root cause of this trigger?" "Am I ready to let this wound heal?"

Every trigger is rooted in a wound within. The wounds of the soul are the entry point for the light to enter. And it is the darkness that brings the light. You either learn the lessons presented to you through life's experiences, or you turn away and perpetuate the learning points throughout your life continuing for 3 generations. Some lessons continue to come back so that you can learn a deeper level. This life is truly one lesson after another. The more you master, your mind, body, and spirit the easier it is. That doesn't mean you won't deal with hard things, simply that the hard things won't be as heavy and won't be carried out for as long. Ancestral trauma isn't just a theory; we now have overwhelming scientific evidence proving fears are passed down in mice at least two generations. This is essentially proof of what the Bible (NIV) says in Numbers 14:18, "The Lord is slow to anger, abounding in love, and forgiving sin and rebellion. Yet he does not leave the guilty unpunished; he punishes the children for the sin of the parents to the third and fourth generation." The parents sin is what I correlate to ancestral trauma. I have experienced this in so many ways.

I want to say it's ironic that I followed the same path that my mom did, but it's not; it makes sense. I tried extremely hard to be nothing like her. Yet, I unknowingly followed her steps to a T. We both worked at the same strip club at the tender age of 18. We both conceived children in a similar debaucherous manner. We both undervalued ourselves and dated many men who didn't see our worth. I believe this was all the result of ancestral trauma. Shame, self-sabotage, and guilt were running my life just as they ran my mother's life. And they led me to make choices that moved me further into darkness and away from the light. Every choice you make is a choice based on either fear or love.

Every decision made in fear brings more experiences to match, and vice versa for the love. We all have light and darkness within. With that said, we are always emitting fear or love vibrations. These frequencies spread through the cosmos and what we put out into the world is what we receive back. For the most part, utterly unconscious, you are all either a Warrior of Light or a Warrior of Darkness at every moment. You choose every second of every day, consciously or unconsciously, to focus your attention on one or the other. That is the side you feed. This is so important to know because most people think they can't and/or do not make a difference in this world. In fact, you are constantly emitting the frequencies that shape the very structure of this world.

Thanks to divine timing, everything I thought I was, deep down inside, emerged far better than I ever imagined. It's been a rough and wild ride to get here.

Transformation is not easy, the overall energy of your childhood is typically the dominate energy you carry. Our outer environment is a pure reflection of our inner environment. If you want a loving, peaceful world, you must create a loving, peaceful internal environment. This starts with the choice and commitment to be a loving, peaceful person. From there, your journey will be unique depending on what your Earth Mission is. Your journey will involve facing your fears. This will happen regardless of what you choose. The only difference is, when you are authentic and open to receiving guidance from your higher power, your suffering will minimize, and you will have fun along the way.

1. RACISM IN THE FAMILY

Racism shaped my identity as a child and made me ashamed of who I was. I grew up in Kenosha, Wisconsin where racism affected everyone's lives and still has a strong impact to this day. As a very young child, I was told my brother and I had the same dad, a Hispanic guy my mom hooked up with, who was violent and Crazy and racist at the time. Even Jose turned his life over to God and was redeemed. That's where I got the last name Garcia. When I was a couple years old, everyone could see that I was very dark, so relatives started calling me negrita.

When I was about seven, I asked my mom why I was brown and why I was called negrita by everyone in the family. In that moment, my mother changed the story I had always been told, and finally shared the truth; well, what I thought was the truth at that time. She said that one night, when she was hanging out at a bar with a bunch of military guys, she was raped in an alley by an unknown man; a black guy. The rapist was my father. The news came to me like a dagger into my heart. I was disgusted and felt horrible for my mother. And I instantly hated my father. *Will I someday become a monster like him? How can she love me? Am I destined to be a horrible person?* I didn't want to be like him, but I didn't know if my father's blood would turn me into a terrible person later in life.

That fear served me by leading me to Jesus when I was about nine years old. My experience at Bible camp led me to start a similar group, so I coordinated with a mentor and got all of my friends to commit to summer Bible camp. Eventually, I became a Bible thumper and poured my entire life into seeking God and recruiting others to do the same. All of this was driven by my panic over becoming a monster, like my dad. Every single fear, trauma, and experience serves a purpose. You have a choice to find that purpose. This may not seem necessary as you experience the effects of your fears, yet it can make a world of difference when you experience a hardship that is out of your control, like

Me at bible camp with a counselor

being victimized or even when you witness crazy stuff happening in society.

When I was in fifth grade, we read *The Diary of Anne Frank*. That book was so moving for me that I once asked my mom, "What would happen if they started hating black people again? Will you hide me?" By then, I knew I was different from my mom and everyone else in my family, and I was terrified of being harmed or murdered. I would lay in bed contemplating where I would hide when the next race war started. To this day, that fear still affects me when I see protests and riots and all the racism happening. All of that hate is rooted in a lack of love.

My anger, fears and destructive behaviors throughout my life were rooted in a lack of self-love. As a kid, I watched my brother and sister spend summers and holidays with their family, but I spent those times by myself because I wasn't accepted; I was the outcast, the one nobody wanted around. So, instead of happy family gatherings and summers with cousins and grandparents, I stayed home alone while my mom worked. It was a lonely existence.

My maternal grandfather, Terrence Girts, was a good Christian man. Unfortunately, he was also a racist. Like my mother, he'd had a difficult life. Abandoned by his family at a young age, he joined the military and later owned a trucking business.

When my skin started to show the shades of my mixed-racial heritage—around the age of three, he disowned my mother and us kids. At first, he had declared us all dead to him, but he had a change of heart after my mother tried to kill herself. Maybe it was guilt and missed opportunities, maybe it was DCFS asking for his help, either way I am grateful he took us in.

After the suicide attempt, my grandfather and his wife, Joyce, took us in. We went from having never seen them to living with them full-time. Our relationship with my grandparents was off and on. Off when I started showing my blackness as a toddler. On when my mother went to jail and DCFS called them to take us. We had to live with them for months while she recovered in the mental hospital. Then, off again after my Uncle Terry killed himself and they moved to a racist town down south. Despite his racist beliefs, my grandfather was kind and loving towards us. My step-grandmother Joyce tried to be kind, but something in her just wouldn't allow her to be loving, like you would expect a grandmother to be. Not surprisingly, my mother had a low-level hate for how Joyce treated her during her childhood and throughout her whole life. My mother actually blamed Joyce for my uncle's suicide. The unfair treatment they received after being abandoned by their birth mother, and then to be abandoned by her father and his family was a low blow.

My grandfather didn't keep his racism under wraps, even when I was in the car with him. His racism was never directed towards me as a kid; instead, it was passive. He would throw racial slurs at anyone who looked different than him, but only from the safety of his vehicle. We would be in the car and my grandpa would get road rage and say, "Fucking niggers, fucking spics!" It was in there, yet it was often directed at others who looked like me, and he only ever expressed those thoughts in anger. All the while, he was unconcerned with how his racial slurs affected me.

Nothing I did was ever good enough for my Joyce, and as a people pleaser that was heartbreaking. In the mid-1990s my grandparents moved to Kentucky. My grandfather said it was his wife, Joyce, who wanted to move, so he just went along with it. All their neighbors were very racist, so I guess they fit right in. Otherwise, why would they choose to move there? That's just who they were. They would allow my brother and sister to visit them there but said that I would get shot if I visited because of my color. That hurt.

There were so many crazy disturbing things that happened within that family. For instance, Joyce, never wanted my mother close with her father. Joyce accused my mom of trying to flirt with her own dad. She masked jealousy and anger with the word of God to make us feel less than. I did everything I could to please Joyce and get on her good side, but it was never enough. She was filled with low-key judgement. There were lots of comments she spewed that made me question my worth and value often. The one that stuck with me the most was when she was preparing me for Bible camp. I wanted to sing a song. We sat at the piano and she asked me to sing to the key. I tried and she said, "Oh, my, you are tone deaf. You may want to choose a new talent to perform." Because of what she said about me, I believed I was tone deaf all the way until my 30s when I realized I actually have a nice voice—it just needed a little practice.

2. THOUGHT PAIN WAS LOVE

By the age of five, I had been abused in every way possible.

From physical and sexual abuse to neglect and racism at the hands of my own family, I have felt the most pain from the people I loved most. Having a long line of mental health disorders in my family, I too was diagnosed with multiple disabilities, and I grew up poor without any role models or people who showed me true love. My past could have crippled me for life, but somehow, I didn't allow it to. Ultimately, even while being full of darkness my Warrior of Light prevailed.

An addict for most of my life, I told myself stories about how alcohol and weed were normal and necessary for me to keep going. My reasoning was simple: At least I didn't smoke crack or do heroin like most of the few family members I knew. God uses addiction in the most miraculous ways. Anything that we give our power away to gives us the ability to reclaim our power. The lower we go vibrationally, the higher the reclamation can take us. Our pain can always be the greatest catalyst for our power-if we choose to turn the pain into power.

When I came into this world, I was surrounded by hurt people who hurt me in more ways than most people can imagine. I thought pain was love, and because of that, throughout most of my life, I felt conflicted. I wanted love desperately but was so afraid of the pain I presumed it came with. When life dealt me one heavy blow after another, I wanted to give up and die; but I didn't. Depending on the day, fear or love pushed me to get up and keep going. Fear isn't all bad, it can motivate. But the more we choose to be guided by love the less fear we will hold onto. The more we release the masks we hold onto, the less fraudulent and fearful we will be.

All humans bring their unhealed traumas into parenthood and really everything they think, say, and do. My mother, Velma LaRue Girts, had a lot of pain, and it shaped everything she did. A gorgeous blonde bombshell, my mother was blessed with a brickhouse body and bright blue eyes that turned hazel depending on her mood. Despite the fact that everyone else saw her beauty, she never could. Every picture I have of her, with few exceptions, revealed a deep pain in her expression. She didn't smile except in a few of her jail house photos (images she took while visiting her incarcerated boyfriends) and one boudoir photo shoot she posed for in her thirties.

Abandoned by both of her parents, she never knew love, so she didn't know how to show it or give it to her own children. She definitely tried her best. By the time she was five, her mother had abandoned her. My mom's biological mother's name was Shirley. Other than her being French, I still do not know much about her. She and my mom reunited when my mom was about thirty-three years old. By this time, Shirley appeared to have either an intellectual developmental disability (IDD) or mental decline. She struggled to hold a conversation, she had body tremors, and she made a lot of interesting sounds. Shirley and Terry (my grandpa) broke up right away and Terry moved on to my mother's stepmom, Joyce.

My mom's father, Terry Girts, Sr., deserted her twice, once when she was a toddler and then again when she was fifteen. At that point, my mother and her only biological brother, Terry Girts, Jr., were put into foster care. Their father and his second wife, Joyce, maintained custody of Joyce's four kids. That was a hurtful blow to my mother. They were not in trouble financially, but my mother and her brother were seen as problem kids, so they were kicked out. My mother went to a group home separate from her brother, thereby feeling abandoned and alone yet again. She was sexually abused and beaten up often in the group homes, so she would run away. She lived on the streets with the bitterness of knowing her father was raising four of Joyce's kids as his own, treating them like the family she wished she had. With that kind of start in life, it's no wonder she struggled as a young adult and mother. The pain she experienced in her life was so horrible, it took her years to reveal to me some of the heartaches and traumas she survived as a child, through her young adult life, and even into her later years.

Not long after that terrible abandonment, my mother got pregnant and gave birth to my sister Letiecia. Two years later, I was born, and eleven months after that, my brother, Joey was born. Shortly after Letiecia was conceived, her father, a Chicano gangster, murdered a guy. Him and his friends beat up a man, tied him to a truck and then dragged him until he died. He went right to prison and my mother soon hooked up with another demented, abusive man, José

Garcia, Joey's father. Jose was an angry man who was also involved with gangs. José hated Letiecia's father with a passion and beat Letiecia and my mother any chance he got.

During one incident, José beat Letiecia for soaking through her diaper. When my mother tried to stop him from harming Letiecia, he beat my mother for interfering. Without a doubt, Letiecia experienced the worst abuse of us all, including sexual abuse. Most of her abusers were unknown to me, but even to this day I am reminded of the abuse every time I run into people who literally tell me stories of that terrible time.

In my early childhood, we lived in a trailer home next to Lake Michigan in Kenosha, Wisconsin. The people around us did whatever they wanted to us. I have a picture of myself around three years old; my brother was two. The adults who claim they were trying to give us a break from our horrid living conditions decided to give us a bong half the size of my brother and taught us how to smoke. If I didn't have a picture of it, I wouldn't have remembered the incident because this was just a normal day growing up.

Me and my brother smoking a bong age 3

In early 1990, I was three and Letiecia, who we called TC, took us on a joyride. Well, almost. She was maybe five and Joey was two. Our parents were sleeping, and TC got the bright idea to steal the car. "Come on guys, we gotta get out of here."

Joey and I jumped up and wearing the same clothes from the day before. We all ran outside, eager to go wherever TC was taking us. She put us in the car, turned the key in the ignition, put the car in gear, and we started rolling backwards. Thank God there was a tree nearby that we backed into. With the car stopped, we just sat there, unsure what to do next. All of a sudden, a neighbor came running towards the car.

"What are you kids doing? Get out of this car!"

She snatched us out of the car, one by one. Then, she marched us back inside the house. But she didn't know the abuse we were running from; or did she? Once inside, she woke my mother up. "Girl, you need to keep an eye on these bad-ass kids of yours," she said. "They were about to drive off in your car."

When José heard that, his face turned red, and he started screaming at us. We ran behind the neighbor, hoping she would protect us, but it didn't help. Despite my mom's efforts to calm him down, José got hold of each of us and beat the crap out of us, especially Letiecia. She always got the worst of everything. There is no way any normal human could withstand all of the mistreatment and abuse she went through and not be affected by it. All of that hurt and violence—being beaten regularly and sexually abused as a toddler, a pre-teen, and even in adulthood—created beliefs and brain patterns that affected everything she did throughout her life. This cycle repeated for her so many times it was unbelievable. They say neglecting or ignoring a kid stunts their growth. This does not mean that she couldn't overcome those traumas, she just had to work much harder to do it. At times she was able to live a healthy life, often short-lived for a couple months at a time. Very early on, TC adopted the same behaviors that had hurt her so much, she eventually became an abuser, with Joey and me as her victims.

Early on, my cousins and sister forced Joey and me to reenact abuses that they had been subjected to. We were directed to play "house". It was a game for us, so we didn't think anything bad of it at the time. While Joey and I played the roles of mom and dad, TC and the older cousins would pair up and make out. Sometimes there would be three of them fingering and dry humping each other. Most of the time, TC did not have to try hard to get Joey and me to participate in her escapades. We were generally eager to do whatever she said because we looked up to her and wanted to be just like her.

She was often in a playful state, but even then, she seemed manipulative, like she was only being nice to get us to do whatever she wanted, like kissing and playing with her private parts. We didn't know how to have sex, but we sure tried. To her, and even to us, this behavior was an expression of love. We wanted to please her, not only because she was our sister, but also because we were afraid of her. Even with all of the love she showed us most of the time, we were deeply afraid to piss her off because her temper was explosive. When she wasn't playful, she was angry. If we didn't do whatever she wanted, she would beat us. So, Joey and I did everything we could not to make her mad.

TC was rough but not as bad as our cousin Raymond. Raymond held a gun to my brother's head and forced him to have sex with his sister, our other cousin. From what I heard, the gun was loaded. That incident proved to me that this world was painful and didn't make any sense. I was so thankful I didn't go to my cousin's house that day. My brother came home differently and told me what happened. He made me promise not to tell anyone, but I told my mom anyway. I feared Raymond, and didn't want to be around him anymore. That didn't matter, eventually the fear wore off because Raymond was a teen, so we had to see him no matter what. Our parents didn't give us choices about where we stayed when we needed a babysitter. We went with whomever took us. Most of the time, the people we were left with were gentler than Letiecia. But when you are faced with daily cruelty, this kind of crap just becomes another normal day.

Joey and I bonded tremendously from a very young age. In fact, we were nearly inseparable as children. As we grew into teenagers, many people thought we were boyfriend and girlfriend because we didn't look related and were always together.

We all grew up amid the unmistakable racism of Kenosha, Wisconsin. It did not take me long to recognize that I was the only one in the family with African American heritage. I didn't look like any of my family members, and really, neither did my sister and brother. But my skin tone was always darker because I was the only one mixed with African American. Not looking like my family always made me feel like I didn't belong. To make matters worse, my mom didn't spend much time with us, so I always felt like we were a burden to her and that we were unimportant. Looking back, I now know that my mother did the best she could.

In any picture I have of myself as a child, it's easy to see that I was unhappy. I hardly ever smiled, neither did anyone in my family except when we were young. All I wanted was attention, but everywhere I turned, people were too busy for me. The only time I was acknowledged was when I was serving them or entertaining them by cleaning the house, massaging them, cooking, or even entertaining them by doing drugs with them.

My mother worked all the time. She had no instructions for how to ensure our safety, and I'm sure she had no idea of the dangers she put us in by leaving us with random neighbors, friends, and family members. She didn't know how to protect us because she was never protected by her family. She taught us to love superficially because that was all she knew. If we had the bare minimum essentials, she felt she was doing a good job as a mom. She always made sure we had a home and that there was food. To her, that was what we needed from her.

We took family photos once, but we never went on a family vacation or camping trip. My mother didn't take us to the park unless she was dropping us off for the entire day. When she dropped us off, we wouldn't know when she was coming back. She didn't have the knowledge or depth to truly love us because she didn't love herself. Without self-love, you cannot show true love to anyone. She wasn't affectionate or caring, like you would expect a mother to be. I didn't realize the absence of love and affection until I saw how other mothers loved and cared for their kids.

My teen photo

A growing jealousy built up in me without me realizing it. I hid this jealousy inside my entire life, stuffing it deep within, knowing it was wrong while not knowing how to process it. As an adult, I finally learned to surrender the jealousy and self-pity as soon as it came up simply by saying, "God, I surrender this jealousy to you. Thank you for freeing me from this." It takes a level of discipline to do this consistently, but it is one of the most rewarding, freeing activities I have done for myself. I later realized that my mom did the best she could with what she had. After all, she was never shown love, so how could she show it to us?

NO LOVE, PEOPLE PLEASING

From as far back as I can remember, I've felt a piercing pain in my heart. At times, it was so sharp it would take my breath away. I noticed it most whenever anyone made fun of me. That teasing was a reminder to me of my reality that I wasn't worthy of love. The agony of not being loved felt like a sharp piercing dagger in my heart. The ache was so severe that at a very young age I vowed I would never bring kids into this world because I thought this torture was normal. That painful hole remained within my heart well into my thirties.

To mask the misery I felt, I resorted to hurting myself in various ways. One by one, I would pull strands of my hair out, or pinch myself, or burn myself, or dig my fingernails into my skin, all to numb the emotional pain I felt constantly. The physical pain distracted me from the pain I felt in my heart. When one form of self-inflicted torture didn't work, I would try another. Any discomfort on the outside felt better than the anguish I felt inside. What I didn't realize then was that the pain I felt inside was the absence of love. I yearned to be loved by someone, anyone. But because I had never experienced true love—from a parent, sibling, or other relative, I didn't really know what love felt like. So, I looked for it outside of me.

At five years old, I would sing the lyrics to "Weak" by the girl group SWV. "I get so weak in the knees, I can hardly speak . . ." I wanted a boyfriend. I wanted someone to love me so the physical and emotional pain would go away. That song talks about being in love with someone who makes you great, a deep love that changes everything for you. I had convinced myself that I was broken, unlovable, or there was something wrong with me, so if I fell in love or if someone loved me, it would change the void and the sting I felt in my heart. I cared about everyone around me and how they felt, but no one did that for me. It was very painful, and I was always hurting. A growing resentment festered, hidden within. Aside from hurting myself physically to detract from the emotional ache I felt, another method I learned was to do things for others with the hope that they would respond with something that felt like love to me. I cleaned the house every day in hopes of receiving a word or gesture of appreciation, attention, or acknowledgment. I became my mom's favorite by doing these things.

I found out later that my mom was a people pleaser, and I realized I had been emulating her practically all my life in this regard. The contrast in her personality was hard to reconcile. On the one hand, she was afraid to speak up for herself with others, most often with work and the men she allowed into her life. On the other hand, when she was home with us kids, she was vicious. She let out on us all the stress and pain from dealing with the day. Her tone of voice and the color of her eyes let me know when she was angry and ready to pounce on us if we did anything wrong. But whenever she was with one of her boyfriends—she never stood up or spoke up for herself. She was voiceless. Because of her pleasing ways she never knew who to say yes to and who to say no to. She had no boundaries. She was so miserable inside that when she took her mask off at home, all the viciousness came out. But there were times she took up for us. Unfortunately, it didn't always end well.

A couple of months before my uncle Terry passed, he came over for a visit one day. I had only met him once before and I was thrilled to see him again. Because my mother didn't keep in touch with her family much, the thought of seeing her brother seemed like the chance to meet a new friend, someone who might fill the void of love within me. I decided to pour my people-pleasing efforts in his direction. At seven years old, I prepared the house as if a dignitary was coming over. I cleaned up and made my favorite mashed potatoes and gravy (the flaky kind) and mac and cheese. When he got there, he came into the kitchen to see what I was doing.

"Is this what you call potatoes?" he asked with a disgusted smirk on his face. "Look at this, there's flakes at the bottom of the pan. That's not how you do it. This is a mess!" he yelled. "If you're gonna do this, do it right."

After all the work I had done to cook for him and clean up the kitchen, he yelled at me because the potatoes weren't perfect. Then, he claimed the kitchen was still dirty. I had washed a sink full of dishes. All he could see was that I hadn't cleaned out the food at the bottom of the sink. Confused and hurt, I ran out of the kitchen crying, disappointed that I had failed to please him. How could he say those things to me, especially after how much work I had put in and how hard I tried to please him? I never wanted to see him again.

When my mom came home, she asked him why I was crying, and he told her what happened. What the fuck? You didn't have to yell at her," she said to him.

She was angry and he knew it. They argued for some time. The louder they screamed at each other, the worse I felt. This was all my fault, and I felt terrible. Crying, I ran outside into the backyard and stayed there until I heard the yelling stop, and I watched Terry storm off in a big, brown, old-school car.

Within weeks after that incident, my uncle hung himself. Of course, I didn't know the details of his suicide; I still don't. I know it involved depression and significant financial debt. I remember going to the funeral and everyone crying. This was my chance to console them all. There I was, running around getting everyone's tissues and rubbing their backs, asking them what they needed and how I could help. I was so busy trying to comfort everyone else, I didn't allow my own grief to show. Because of that, my brother, sister, and mom were mad at me. How could I be there amid all that grief and not be crying like everyone else? At the time, I didn't feel anything. The initial shock of hearing about his death did not produce tears for me. After all, I had only met him twice, and the last time I saw him, he was mean to me. Any emotion I felt at the time was for the other family members who grieved his loss.

My people-pleasing persona caused me to do things I thought would make others happy, even though I didn't really want to do those things. No matter what they asked, in that moment, my mind would immediately think that I had to do it, otherwise they may not like me. This continued well into my adult life and built up a scab of misery and resentment towards others but mostly directed at myself. The feeling often felt like rage within. Often, I would get so overwhelmed and resentful it felt like my blood would boil over the smallest things. Once I felt heated, the mental overload would ramp up with psychotic thoughts. *Who do you think you are, Theresa? No one loves you and no one likes you. Everyone hates you. You are a stupid nigger. Not even the niggers like you.* I hated my nose, my hair, and my thin, boyish body. I hated the fact that all of the people around me went on vacation and no one invited me. I hated how lonely and desperate I felt for anyone to give 1 fuck about me. Even more, I hated everything I had to do to get anyone to notice me. From there, a spiral of depressive thoughts would form and the feeling that I was a disappointment would rise within me.

Doing things to please others distracted me from my own unhappiness. If I was focused on making someone else happy, I didn't prioritize my need for love and the pain I felt inside. Like other people pleasers, I did it unconsciously, unaware that I was avoiding my own pain by trying to fix the world around me. By pleasing others, I didn't have to deal with the mess inside of me. Doing for others kept me digging the hole of dissatisfaction within myself. If you know you are a people pleaser, I highly recommend going into silent retreats with yourself on a regular basis. Silent retreats are simply 1-72 hours of being in pure silence with no outside demand. Start small and build your way up. Many silent retreat centers will give you a whiteboard to walk around with so you can still write, read and be in silence. The idea is to stay away from phones, tv's, computers and any other electrical noise that could interfere. In the silence, you will see what your mind is clinging to, and you will be able to see your true nature. In the silence, God works wonders within us. The wonders may not be seen but with consistency, you develop a deep relationship with Source. Source is always talking to you, the moment you reach to God, God is there. This is one of the greatest, cheapest gifts we can give ourselves. Start with deciding to go silent. Tell whoever is in the household so they are prepared to leave you alone. Write down any repetitive thoughts. The next day, reflect on the thoughts and take conscious action towards releasing them. A simple free way is to surrender your findings to God or creating your own ritual of release. There are many books on sacred ceremonies, Reverand Ahriana Platten, PHD wrote a fantastic book/guide called *Rights and Rituals: Harnessing the Power of Sacred Ceremony*. Please remember—whatever process you are guided to do will be perfect. You may be guided to create your own, play with it knowing you are supported and guided by your Divine Higher Self. A simple ritual is writing down what you wish to release and then burning it in a safe way depending on safety measures for your specific location. Unity Spiritual Centers often have release ceremonies if you want to do a free sacred release in a group setting. My streamlined favorite way to release negative programing is with Psych-k. It is a powerful, proven technique I use to help myself and my clients release limiting beliefs in moments. No matter what your background is, you will feel a shift and it will be profound. Remember to replace negative beliefs with positive new beliefs. Anything you release creates more space within, so replace it with something lightful.

INTUITION

From as far back as I can remember, I could easily anticipate the thoughts and actions of those around me. For instance, I could sense that my mom was thirsty before she said anything, and I would offer to get her a drink. Intuitively, I knew when she was close to home or on her way home even though I hadn't spoken to her for hours. I knew when she was lying to me, and I would point out the holes in her stories.

Because of this unexplainable insight, I could not accept answers or reasoning from others for their decisions when I knew in my gut that they were not telling the truth. I couldn't help myself in my pursuit of truth and understanding. Still, after endless questions, and explanations that never answered those questions, nothing really ever made sense to me. I knew in my heart that there had to be more to life than what I was witnessing. To this day, it takes consistent effort to keep my intuitive gifts in balance. This is because when you experience a lot of trauma, your ego can mimic your intuitive guidance, and it often sounds like the same voice. This is where spiritual discernment comes from. If you are struggling with discernment, clear your vessel. Water fasting is one of the fastest ways to do this. Ask God to bless the fast and do not whine about it. Address fasting with excitement for the guaranteed clarity that is on its way, and you will have more ease and grace during your fast. The more you complain, the less you benefit and the harder it is. Start to pay attention to how you feel when you are developing. Are you developing from a place of fear or love? Your motivation will always influence the outcome.

Paying attention to my feelings has been the greatest gift to increasing my awareness. The more aware we are, the more present we are. This is a key difference that helped me create a bit of space between myself and the things my family subjected me to. I was the hyper-sensitive child who felt resentment constantly. The pain of unhealed emotions would rage through my body. When I was in a mood, look out world I was taking it out on every single person I met. At a very young age, I had muscle tension and carried stress in my shoulders, head, and back like a grown woman. By the Grace of God, I was able to view their actions as opportunities for me to learn. What I saw in them made me certain that I didn't want to be like them, so I decided to make my own way by running in the opposite direction. For instance, none of my family did well in school. I knew they were ignorant.

Because of that, I chose to learn as much as possible at a young age so I could have a better life. Because of my determination to learn, I easily excelled in school.

I saw how the men my mother dated beat her up and treated us like crap, so I vowed to never date a man like that. I wondered why she dated losers and never had much time around healthy, loving men. Many times, I would ask my mom what she saw in the men she dated and why she let them treat her so badly. Not surprisingly, she would get pissed and push me away. I don't even think she knew why she fell for those losers. And it wasn't only her boyfriends that treated her like crap, it was also her friends. She had so many friends that used her and stole from her, and they always smoked her weed and left. Every single one of my judgments came true in my own life despite my vows. My mother was intuitive and could see a friend or guy of mine and knew right away whether they would be good to me or not.

How is it that she sees through my crappy friends but not hers?

One thing I never understood until writing this book was how my mom was gorgeous and never knew it. I would watch her stand in the mirror and complain about her face, her belly, her legs, and just be totally confused about how she couldn't see her own beauty. Everyone around me thought my mom was drop-dead gorgeous. One time, a boy I was crushing on in high school asked me for my number and then asked me my mother's name since he intended on hitting on my mother. *Why doesn't she see her own beauty?* She couldn't see it because she was blinded by negative thinking.

The beautiful Velma LaRue Girts

All the questions I asked became an unknown superpower for me. I am not special. I am simply curious and determined to be my greatest self. I didn't realize at the time, but asking questions in the form of "I wonder" statements contribute to a child-like curiosity that opens you to receive answers quickly. The answers usually come shortly after the question and they come in the form of undeniable synchro-divinities—seemingly unrelated awe-inspiring experiences that propel you into moments, a period or a lifetime of unimaginable love, joy and success. These signs and "out of this world" synchronicities gave me an internal compass, offered me a haven of purity and truth—something that couldn't be shamed or stripped away—and enabled me to find silver linings in the darkest of moments.

Although that intuition provided a kind of armor, it also became a weight on my shoulders, causing me to be consumed with trying to understand and help others with their pain. Because of that, I lost sight of myself. Putting myself first and safeguarding my own well-being wasn't even on my radar. If someone else had a need, I would give everything I had to them, not reserving enough for my own wants and needs. I had an abundant well of empathy, for everyone and everything except myself.

VIOLENCE AT HOME

Growing up being abused and neglected, it took work and commitment to learn to love myself. Unconditional love was ambiguous and completely foreign. While learning, I fell for all kinds of things that were better than the unfathomable abuse and neglect I had experienced.

In fact, my father Charles Brownlee (you'll learn more about him later) was my mother's sugar daddy. He had won the lottery, and with his winnings bought her two side-by-side trailers—one we called home, the other she called work. She essentially used the "office" next door to make a few dollars off other prostitutes and to sell herself. I got this information as an adult, hearing my mother tell stories of her past while she was drunk. Of course, I have memories of my own.

Our environment was very violent, and all that brutality made an indelible mark on my psyche. In my childhood years, I witnessed various kinds of abuse, from watching my mother be verbally and physically abused by her lovers, to seeing her fighting girls outside of the trailer. I was always afraid of my mom when she got angry. Just as I had come to accept the stabbing pain in my heart as normal, I began to believe that violence was an ordinary part of everyday life. My mom went to jail for being involved in a brawl. That experience caused her to do a 180-degree turnaround with her life. The change started with her leaving José Garcia, my little brother's dad. He was furious. It took some time for her to work up the nerve to do it, but once she made the move to leave, all hell broke loose.

In the weeks following the breakup, we were all on high alert, believing José would kill us if he had the opportunity because he'd often said he would. He and his gang buddies loved to hurt people. One night, as we drove down Sheridan Road, we came to a halt at a stop sign. Out of nowhere, Joe jumped onto the hood of the car and started hitting the windshield screaming, "I will kill you, you stupid bitch. I will kill all of you!"

My mother sped away and yelled out the window, "Fuck you--You stupid mother fucker!" Suddenly, she slammed her foot on the break, stopping the car. Joe went flying off the car and onto the pavement. Then, my mother sped away, cursing under her breath and glancing behind us nervously, as if Joe could get up and run after the car.

She drove us to the house of one of her friends. She couldn't risk taking us home; he would find us there. As soon as we burst through her friend's front door, my mom dragged Letiecia, Joey, and me into the kitchen and shoved us into the cabinets underneath the counter. "You stay there and shut up," she said. "Don't say a word or else he will find you." I was terrified and certain that we were all going to die that night. Curled tightly in a ball beneath the kitchen sink, I tried to breathe as quietly as possible. Thank God David showed up just before Joe broke into the house. David had a huge family and was ready to protect my mother and us. About an hour later, Joe arrived. When he saw David there, he knew he wouldn't win, so he left like a coward.

Shortly after that, we moved into a homeless shelter. That's when my mother met Zodie, a beautiful six-foot tall, strong, Southern black woman with about ten kids. By this time, some of her kids were grown and on their own, and there were three living with her: Tati (who was my sister's age) Jazz, and Punky. Zodie and my mother hit it off instantly. That first night at the shelter, Zodie asked my mother why she was there. When Zodie found out that my mother had a home, she said, "Fuck this shelter girl, I will help you fuck that nigga up if he comes ova!"

It was easy to believe Zodie because she had a fierceness about her. Muscles were genetic in Zodie's family. Even Punky, who was two, had well-defined arms that looked like a toddler who did hundreds of pushups a day. It was crazy. The next day, Mom and Zodie gathered all of us kids and we went back to the trailer. As soon as we got there, Zodie filled a pot with oil and my mom asked her what she was making. Zodie replied, "Let this nigga come in and this hot grease will be ready for him!" Shortly after we were settled back into the trailer, José came by in a rage. He was so angry and crazy that he dove headfirst through the window. As promised, Zodie quickly threw the pot of hot grease on him, then hit him with the pan. He screamed and ran out the door in obvious pain. For years after that, we did not see or hear anything from José.

THE STORIES I TOLD MYSELF

With Jose out of the picture, my mom quickly turned her attention and affections to the next man. With David being her hero, I can see why she turned to him. When I was four years old, we moved into David's apartment on Lake Michigan. He lived in a four-unit complex with multiple complexes stacked. All the people in that building were either abusive or/and addicts. The apartment next to ours had a racist murderer who beat his wife and kids all the time. Other neighbors and my sister and her friends would molest each other and, at times, molest my brother and me. A lot of David's nieces and nephews lived there, and many of them sexually abused us kids. They were nice people, yet they perpetuated the same sexual abuses they had experienced, most likely from David's brother, who molested nearly all the kids in the family. It puzzles me to this day how many wives and families protect their family child molesters. We need to stand up for our kids and protect them first. My sister Letiecia would meet the boy next door under the stairs, and they would have threesomes. It is mind blowing to write this because now I see how crazy it is. At the time, though, I saw being molested as a form of playing "Mommy and Daddy" in a trauma-driven mad house. For anyone that survived childhood sexual abuse, Finding Our Voices is an incredible non-profit that provides all kinds of free support in the form of healing workshops and art. It is important that we share these experiences, and many families do not provide the forum. Even if you believe all your family members are safe, regularly ask your kids questions and give them many opportunities to speak up and tell you what is going on in their world. If you notice sleeping issues or your kid's withdrawal from a family member, get lovingly curious.

Despite all the sexual abuse, David was a good man and never sexually abused us kids. He did his best to be a decent role model for us kids. The problem was, he was an alcoholic, which led him to be emotionally abusive towards my mom and us kids. He would do it in a playful way, completely unaware of the damage he was causing. One day, everyone was home, and I was having fun jumping on our new bed (all of us kids shared a bed until we were much older). David came in and told me to sit in the living room with everyone else. He stood in front of my family and started mocking me, saying, "My name is Buckwheat, and I only eat mashed potatoes and gravy, chicken noodle soup, and butter and jelly sandwiches." Hearing him call me Buckwheat infuriated me. I had been called Buckwheat throughout my life, and because of that, I hated my own blackness. That teasing felt akin to being called a nigger. My blood began to boil, and I punched him in the nose.

He started bleeding instantly, then yelled for my mom to whoop my ass. She said, "No, you shouldn't make fun of her." I was both shocked and relieved that my mother had my back. It felt so good to get him back and to have my mom stick up for me.

As a child, I knew something was wrong with David. Back then, I just called him mean and crazy. As an adult, I can realize David had some serious money blocks and food insecurities. He would monitor the refrigerator to make sure we didn't eat too much, or we didn't eat anything he claimed to be only for him. Although we weren't allowed to eat any of the snacks my mother and David bought for themselves, we were allowed to eat the basics: cereal, bread, bologna, rice, and sliced cheese. Even our consumption of the basics was monitored. That scarcity of food undoubtedly led me to create limiting beliefs about myself.

Most of the interactions I had with adults were based on discipline—basically me being yelled at or getting spanked—or me giving and trying to please others. I wasn't asked what I wanted to do for fun with my mom or father figures. We didn't play games or have adventures other than David's family gatherings. At those gatherings, the kids were in one area and the adults were in another partying. I unconsciously believed that other people were more important and deserving than I was. This may be another reason why I spent most of my life putting the needs of other people before mine. This kind of behavior was normalized in my home. Behaviors that are normalized in the home become the lens through which we perceive our reality.

Another story I created from my environment is that food is limited. Because I was hungry so much of the time during my early childhood, I developed strong fears around food that led to interesting behaviors. Food hoarding, over-packing, over shopping, thoughts of doomsday, and worrying about my next meal were constant thoughts and behaviors for me during my twenties and thirties, a time when my schedule was packed with busy-ness. These thoughts added all kinds of extra hurdles to my already hectic life. Whether it is drinking, smoking, sex, shopping, gossiping, tearing others down or building others up, everything is meant to have a natural order. Our actions are determined by what we believe and how we perceive reality. The reality is unless we reflect regularly, we are rather unconscious of most behaviors and ways of thinking. Reflection is important, and at the same time, too much can lead to depression.

Reflecting on my childhood, I realized that my mother lived out a similar theme of never having enough. After a while, I began to see how this played out in her actions. She always put the needs of her friends and the men she was with before her own. Later in life, she expressed that she never felt like she deserved good things. From the moment I heard her say that I knew that was my issue too. Science has proven that trauma is genetic, passed down in DNA, often from patterns that have been unrecognized and unaddressed. It is important to reflect on life and realize the themes and patterns you see generationally so you can learn and grow from them.

Otherwise, you will suffer the pain of unconsciously repeating them.

What parents wouldn't want their child to leap over obstacles they themselves struggled with? The best way to help your kid learn from your experiences is to discuss them; all of them. Learning from good behaviors is easy. Learning from things that you would rather hide is probably the hardest yet most rewarding endeavor. No one wants to talk about suicide; however, my family couldn't hide the fact that we all had depression. Moreover, all the family I grew up with either killed or attempted to kill themselves. How can something that is so ugly and rampant go unspoken of in my household? My mother's father struggled with depression and suicidal thoughts his entire life. With minimal reflection, it is easy to see the cycles throughout my family's generations.

Everyone around me wanted to kill themselves and I wanted to kill myself too. Thoughts of hopelessness flooded my mind constantly, and I remember thinking, *I know when I am older my life will be better.* I also wondered, *Am I going to have this pain inside forever? If I am, then I just want to be done. I will never bring a child into this miserable broken world.* My mother said similar things time and time again. "I'm so sick of being sick and tired. Will it ever fucking stop? It's always fucking something!" She would say that to my sister and my brother all the time. They didn't bat an eye when my mother yelled at them, but each time she yelled at me it broke my heart. I tried very hard to please her to avoid this.

Because I anticipated her needs and did whatever my mom requested, I was perceived as the golden child. At school, I did my work. Unlike my Letiecia and Joey, I didn't get kicked out of elementary school. Middle school was another story and of course I made the most out of that expulsion. At home, I cleaned and helped my mom when I could. But no matter what I did, I couldn't take away the hurt and pain she felt—mentally, emotionally, and physically.

There were times when I felt like she couldn't stand me being near her unless I was massaging her feet or tickling her hair. I now know that she simply needed alone time because she worked so hard as a certified nurse assistant and hospice worker. It drained her. When she came home from working her two jobs, she was completely spent. Most nights, she was so tired she couldn't even look at us. She would walk in the house holding her head with a headache, clearly suffering from terrible pain. From my earliest memories, I felt that she didn't want us. Little did I know it wasn't about us. Instead of talking to us, like most parents would do with their kids, she would go straight to her room and lock the door. Within minutes, we could hear her crying, and then the smell of weed would seep through the crack beneath the door.

She was holding on to years of trauma from her life and ancestry, years of trying and failing and wanting to give up, of loving and not being loved back, of wanting better for herself but not knowing how to get it. She was in a lot of physical pain. She constantly experienced pain in nearly every part of her body— her muscles, stomach, and head. Now that I have walked the journey of a similar experience, I wonder if she Had parasites? Some indications of parasites are restless sleep, sweet cravings, digestion issues, low energy and inflammation. My mom was always in pain, and she tossed and turned all night while gritting her teeth. Parasites mess with your nervous system, so hyperactivity is another sign. My mother's daily diet lacked nutrition. She lived on Little Debbie cakes, mayonnaise and cheese sandwiches, and diet Coke. Parasites cause you to have severe cravings, and when you have an unhealthy gut, your body becomes a breeding ground for all kinds of dis-ease. At times, I would be able to get into her room and try to comfort her with a massage, but I could barely use any pressure because her whole body would be so inflamed and tender to the touch. During those moments, she would cry about how tired she was.

After my uncle killed himself, my mom was so depressed that again she wanted to give up and die. Sadly, that hopelessness infected my sister, my brother, and me. We all wanted to die. With the cloud of depression hanging over her head, and after an attempted suicide, my mom admitted herself to a psychiatric facility. That's the second time my grandparents took us in, it only lasted about month. Shortly after going to live with them, my sister started her suicide attempts around the age of ten. Letiecia's suicide attempts started with overdosing on medication. Then, after a couple of those attempts failed, she began slitting her wrist. The suicide attempts continued multiple times over the following ten years.

IF YOU DON'T KNOW WHO YOU ARE, YOU DON'T KNOW HOW TO CARE FOR YOU YET

In the late 1980s and early 90s, we didn't have Google to research how to love and care for ourselves. There were Guru's and cults but not many life coaches or self-improvement workshops in small towns. Most people didn't even know that we needed to learn these things. In the ghettos of Kenosha, Wisconsin, reading books and learning personal development were not normal behaviors. Fleshy living—living out of fleshly desires (numerous sex partners with lots of drugs and alcohol) were normal modes of being in Kenosha.

We all blindly repeat the same stories of our past until we examine those stories and learn. Unless you have someone to show you another way, your chances of understanding how to love yourself and discern life's circumstances are hindered. Humans and animals tend to be just like the beings they grew up with. As children, our perceptions are shaped by our environment, which tells us what behavior is acceptable and what is not. Once we become adults, it is up to us to figure out what is true for us. In a culture riddled with egoic pursuits, truth—just like unconditional love—can be hard to identify. We identify truth by being truth. That means embodying truth with everyone you are in contact with along with yourself. There is no such thing as a white lie, white lies give grounds for confusion and lies to come back to you. We get what we put out. Even if we have examples of honest living, unless we question ourselves, we have no clue of all of the ways our ego creates stories to distort the truth. If you are in a community that is riddled with drugs, abuse, neglect, poverty, and addictions as a way of life, even if the extremes bother you, those behaviors are repeated in all kinds of unique ways.

I created this belief while deciphering Plato's Allegory of the Cave. I first learned about this story while studying for a course in philosophy in college. It blew my mind and instantly changed my life. In this symbolic story, Plato paints a picture of three prisoners chained to a wall since birth. After a while, the three prisoners develop a language and games. For their entire lives, all they see is this wall with shadows. Behind them is a raised wall with a fire. There are people walking behind them with different objects and so the fire creates the shadows they see on the wall. Since they are chained to the wall, they can only see what is in front of them. They believe the shadows talk and make the noises they hear. They develop a game of guessing the shadows.

One day, a man frees one of the prisoners. The prisoner sees the fire for the first time, and it burns his eyes since all he knows is darkness. He tries to turn away and the man drags him outside. The sun hurts even more, but once he begins to see the birds, the trees, the ocean, and the sky, he runs back to free his friends. His friends are playing the shadow game, and he tries to describe the world they are missing. They can't comprehend what he is saying because they have nothing to relate his ambiguous descriptions with. He is literally speaking a new language to them. They assume he is crazy and vow to kill anyone who tries to free them because they do not want to be crazy like him.

Even before I read this story, I knew that my entire life was a lie and that there must be so much more in this world. Once I studied this allegory, I knew that I wanted to know and seek truth. Eventually, I learned a process to decipher truth inwardly first, but that came later in my adult life.

I chose the hard way of self-development early on. Guided by my higher self at the beginning, my ego eventually took the driver's seat without me realizing it. When ego is in the driver's seat, you best believe its main goal is to keep you small and in the sameness. Therefore, it creates a myriad of distractions and disorders to confuse you into staying small. The ego is a blessing, everything created was done for a reason. It helped me uncover unimaginable strength and dependency on God to guide my life. When God—your higher self—is in charge, things are simple and feel good. It took years of discovery before I found the streamlined version I will share with you below. To do this, I use muscle testing. I essentially ask myself questions and I receive instant feedback. We are essentially bundles of information and with minimal training, we all can learn to communicate with our bodies.

My process to uncover the truth in challenging situations is simply to ask my higher self these questions:

1. Is this action or guidance internally motivated?
2. Is this guidance rooted in truth or trauma?
3. Would it be best to act on this now or later?

It is so important I must repeat—we must be truth to know and feel truth. If we are refusing to face a single truth, we will struggle to discern between truth and trauma. They will sound and feel the same and that will create more chaos in your life.

TEASING, SCHOOL, AND MRS. KRUEGER

At school, I always felt left out. I was one of 2 or 3 mixed girls at my school and instead of uniting, we chose to compete. Clicks of friends were formed by race primarily. My dark skin was unmistakable. Because of my dark skin, I was called "Oreo" because I was "black on the outside and white inside." It was another way for them to call me soft.

Racial slurs echoed through my life, an ever-present reminder that I was different. Growing up, it seemed that I was always fighting for a scrap of attention, reluctantly given. Despite that, I was the golden child in the family. I tried the hardest and I gave our mother the most grace. This was just another thing that set me apart from my siblings, inviting a mixture of jealousy and resentment. It was survival of the fittest in our household. Alliances could be formed and shattered in an instant between my siblings and me. The slurs they flung at me— "monkey," "nigger bitch," and others— weren't just verbal weapons but manifestations of their inner racism, which I too had.

We loved to make fun of each other's dads too. Nearly every argument involved racial, and father disses. One time, my brother and I were fighting. I can't remember what started it, but I know that he was chasing me with a knife. Knife fights were normal behavior in my home. My poor mother had to replace countless doors because if we couldn't get the person, we would stab through the door in pure rage.

We were in the kitchen when Joey yelled, "I am going to fuck you up you nigger bitch. You are just like your rapist nigger dad."

"Well at least my dad isn't a wetback murderer," I yelled back. "You're going to be just like that piece of shit!"

Joey grabbed a knife and started chasing me. I ran only a few feet and then turned around and pushed him into the glass kitchen table. His head hit the corner and my heart sank. I thought I had killed him. I screamed as blood began gushing out of his head. My mother was running an afternoon school program at the time. I immediately left the house and ran for five blocks to get to her. When I arrived, I ran into the gym screaming, "I killed him! I'm so sorry, I killed him!" Joey was rushed to the emergency room and ended up having some brain damage and stitches. I felt so bad. If there was a bright side, it was that he stopped chasing me with knives.

At school, the situation was no better. My neediness for friends and attention was probably what caused me to be the oddball and the focus of bullying from my classmates. I felt like everyone always made fun of me, so I deeply yearned for any attention that did not involve me being the brunt of a joke or name calling. Because of that, I turned my efforts to school and tried to get attention from teachers by playing the teacher's pet. I volunteered anytime the teachers asked for help. I worked hard on my homework because good grades felt like approval to me and got me attention. It worked all the way through fourth grade. My excellent grades gave me a spotlight among teachers and students that I appreciated.

By the time I reached fifth grade, things were different. My fifth-grade teacher was Mrs. Krueger, and from day one I could tell she hated me. Her attitude towards me was one of disgust, but I could never figure out why. She looked at me with such distaste. She was probably in her forties—kind of chubby, with dark, short hair, and wire-framed glasses. On any given day, she came to class with an extra-sour look on her face. Whenever she spoke to me, that "bitch face" got even worse. There was nothing I could do to please her, but I tried until she gave me every reason to just give up.

I was usually the first to raise my hand whenever Mrs. Krueger asked a question. By the second month of school, she became annoyed by this. At first, she would ignore me, rolling her eyes and glancing over my head, then calling out to the class, "Anyone other than Theresa?" Heartbroken and embarrassed, I would lower my hand and my head and sit quietly in my seat, often forcing myself to pass out until lunchtime. My friends and I liked to get high, so the next best thing was to breathe heavily and press our hands into our necks to cut off circulation. We would pass out and feel high. It was my favorite way to pass time in her class.

The next day, I'd raise my hand again hoping she would call on me. Again and again, I'd be shut down by Mrs. Krueger. I'm sure the other students noticed, but they had no incentive to speak up. Eventually, I began to get a thrill out of knowing I had the power to piss her off by merely being in the room. Instead of trying to please her, I began to enjoy pissing her off. It was so easy to get her riled up. All I had to do was yell out an answer when no one else spoke up, or chuckle whenever someone else responded. That tit-for-tat became the highlight of my day and it only got worse the more I learned to cover my hurt feelings with volatile and erratic behaviors.

Well before fifth grade, I had started flirting with boys. Because I was so hungry for love, I always wanted a boyfriend. I was good at getting boyfriends, often attracting one boy, getting bored with him, and eventually dumping him for his friend. I got a thrill out of the drama and cruelty of doing this. Like most kids, I was influenced by MTV videos and TV programs that showed woman using their sexiness to get what they want from men. I wanted to have that kind of influence over boys, so I played around with different identities that made me feel special.

One day I came to school with my sister's long blonde ponytail clipped into my dark brown hair. It was super obvious that it was fake and yet I didn't care. Mrs. Krueger asked each student in class to share what they wanted to be when they grew up. When my turn came, I stood up enthusiastically and with a big smile said, "I want to be just like Anna Nicole Smith." Mrs. Krueger stared at me with her mouth open and eyes bulging in disbelief. As I turned to sit down, I flipped my ponytail like I was a valley girl from the movie "Clueless." The ponytail, which was not secure, flew across the room. Three boys, eager to come to my rescue, suddenly jumped out of their seats and dove for the weave. Crashing in a heap on the floor, they began to fight.

"Stop it right now!" Mrs. Krueger yelled.

As the scuffle continued, she called for security and the principal came. You would think I would have been embarrassed as we marched to the principal's office, but I wasn't. The shock for me was that my brother, Joey, was already with the principal when she came to my class. He was either fighting, smoking, or up to some other shenanigans. Angry and disappointed, the principal forcefully led Joey by his shirt and me by my ear into her office and called our mother. She caused Joey's shirt to rip. Less than an hour later, my mother came in furiously, first at us for misbehaving, and then at the principal because she had torn Joey's shirt in her heavy-handed haul into her office. When my mother saw me crying and Joey's torn shirt, she lost it and smacked the principal in the face. Joey and I were both suspended after that, and my mother was issued a citation for misdemeanor assault. Following that incident, the principal was very nice to us and never again put her hands on us. Years later, that same principal was assigned to the middle school I attended and played a pivotal role in supporting me during those formative years.

After the ponytail event, Mrs. Krueger started to completely ignore me. I pretty much hated her by then, so it wasn't a big deal. But her rejection severed any interest I had in school. Teachers have powerful potential to ignite or disempower kids. With no oversight or interest in my schoolwork at the classroom level, I started skipping school, which led to me hanging out with a very troubled young woman named Vera. Vera, who was about eighteen years old, was friends with my sister at first and lived alone in a house about five blocks from us. Both of her parents had died in a tragic accident, leaving her alone and depressed, just like the people in my family. She was also an addict, who smoked weed and drank liquor like so many of the adults I was used to being around. Because drugs and alcohol had been a normal part of my household since I was very young, I was eager to partake with Vera and felt grown when I did.

This was the same time that my sister, Letiecia started giving Joey and me "CAPS," a date-rape drug also known as GHB (gamma hydroxybutyrate). Letiecia had this theory that if she made us do whatever drugs she did, we wouldn't tell on her. She was right. The fear I felt of my mother's wrath while partaking in the drugs prevented me from snitching on my sister. I took note of her manipulation techniques every step of the way. As for her friend Vera, I looked up to her. She was beautiful, and she reminded me of the singer

Gwen Stefani, whose music we loved. I was drawn to Vera's independence, so I went along with whatever she did.

Vera had a baby whose daddy was a partier. Among his crew was a guy named Adam, who I had a big crush on because he was hot and seemed sweet. He was about eighteen years old, and he rented a room on the second floor of Vera's house. At ten years old, before I even knew what love was, I fell in love with Adam, a childhood kind of love that was more infatuation. Every day I thought about him, imagining the things we would do together and how I wanted him to treat me. By then, I was nearing my eleventh birthday. Vera told me that if I wanted to keep Adam, I should have sex with him.

Without hesitation, I took her advice.

One night after a party where we were drinking Southern Comfort and smoking weed, I lost my virginity. After drinking too much, I went outside to puke. Adam followed me out and held my hair while rubbing my back, then he led me to his room to recover. As I melted to the floor, exhausted from the puking ordeal, our encounter began. In no time, he had pulled my shirt over my head and then began unzipping my jeans. He started by kissing and rubbing me, then progressed to using his fingers. It all happened so fast, and with each part of my body he touched, I felt closer to him. I had a deep desire to touch and be touched. I even purposely would breathe at his pace to feel closer. *Is this what love feels like?*

The experience was awkward and unclear. He grabbed a towel from a corner of the room and spread it out on the floor, then guided me to lie on my back on top of the towel. When he penetrated me, I wanted to scream because it hurt so badly. The pain of that experience was mortifying and brought tears to my eyes, but I tried to hide it by pretending I enjoyed it. I was afraid that he would leave me if he thought I didn't like it, so I endured. By the time he finished, the towel beneath me was soaked in blood. I was too young to realize that this was normal for someone losing her virginity, and I was ashamed for having made such a mess.

In the days and weeks after that encounter, I became more and more obsessed with Adam. I thought about him all the time and called him every day. He was super loving and attentive at first. Our initial sexual encounters were actually molestation because I was so young and inexperienced. He was kind and gentle, yet I didn't know what I was doing, and he was twice my age. We hung out heavy for a few weeks. Then, suddenly, Vera lost her home from not paying the mortgage or taxes, moved far away, and I hardly saw her again.

Of course, when Vera moved, Adam had to move too, so he found a place with one of his friends. Suddenly, he didn't answer or return my calls. I was heartbroken. He had ghosted me and that stabbing pain in my heart returned. I felt lost, sick and alone. The pain I felt was unbearable. My fragile emotional state couldn't stand the rejection. I wanted to die, but I wanted to be with him even more. There was no way I would take his dismissal as a final act to end our relationship. I was convinced that I would see Adam again. For months, I wore his T-shirt nearly every day in a dramatic statement of solidarity with him. With each phone call he didn't answer, I hoped even harder that he would come back to me.

Thankfully, Veronica, my older "cousin," who was one of our neighbors, helped distract me from the pain I felt from Adam's rejection. Veronica was a beautiful voluptuous blonde with a petite body. She lived down the street from me, and I stayed at her place so much that I practically lived there. I would cook, clean, and babysit. She paid me and would take me out to party with her. She kept me supplied with weed and when we went out, she got me in the bars and would always find coke. She preferred Hispanic bars. Drinking sex on the beach we would dance with guys, do coke and party all night. At the time, I was only thirteen years old. Veronica was a traumatized young lady who was looking for love in all the wrong places just like me.

Veronica's baby's daddy was not very involved at the time. However, his nephew, Bamm was over there a lot. He was tall, dark, and handsome, but quiet. He never spoke to me. I saw that as a challenge, so I threw myself at him. In no time, we were hooking up. He said he had an older girlfriend who took care of him financially, so he wasn't interested in me. After some time with me, that changed. He became interested and we both believed we were in love.

3. LOOKING FOR LOVE IN ALL THE WRONG PLACES

I flirted with literally everyone. My 6th grade teacher Mrs. Palmer was right when she called me a hussy. I was a bit thirsty for attention. Still as a teacher, she should not have said that about a kid in front of the class. Any adult should know that if you see a child trying to get ridiculous amounts of attention, try getting to know them and find out why. Most likely, they are being abused and/or neglected at home. Everyone likes to make fun of these kids or teens, calling them hoes and often expecting them to become teen moms. Can you imagine how schools would change if all teachers believed that each student was a Divine expression? I wonder what would happen if all teachers knew that they themselves were an expression of the Divine and that they truly had the power to pour life into each kid they encounter? I know many incredible teachers who truly believe in their students and their ability to positively impact their students. I can't help but wonder what would happen if all teachers were given the tools and resources to be their truest self so that they could teach the kids by example. When we stand in our full authentic power, everyone around us is vibrationally uplifted because of it. I wonder what would happen if we saw a radical shift in child-directed classes? I wonder if this could be the catalyst to help kids enjoy learning more.

At the end of the day, my behaviors were rooted in deep neglect and abuse. I just wanted to feel loved and like I was important to someone. Without knowing what true love is, lust and attention felt like love to me.

At home, things just kind of always sucked. My mom worked day and night, so she was never home to care for us like a typical mother would. Even then, I knew she was doing her best. I hit puberty around the age of thirteen. I became very mean, and I was angry at everyone. It seemed like no one gave a shit about me or anything that was happening in my life. I was beginning to see that our home life wasn't normal, and it seemed nobody was doing anything about it. Every time I thought about it, I wanted to hurt someone, including myself. Even something as seemingly simply as having food in the refrigerator became a source of trauma in our home.

One day, Joey came home from school and went straight to the kitchen in search of food. He had left for school without eating breakfast because there was no food. At school he had lunch, but we did not get snacks. He was angry and began opening and closing all the cabinets, then the refrigerator door. There was nothing except three eggs, powdered milk, and a couple of other things, but definitely nothing fancy or even appetizing for dinner.

"Is there any fucking food in this fucking house?" he screamed. He wasn't talking to anyone in particular.

Letiecia and I were there, but my mom was away, working, as usual. We were all hungry, but there was nothing we could do about it. We had no money to buy anything, so we just sat there with our stomachs growling, hoping our mom would come home with some food.

Frustrated and desperate, Joey called 911 to tell them we had no food. Calling them only made matters worse for my mom. As it turned out, she happened to stop at the grocery store for food on her way home from work that night. She got there with a few more items, like bread and cereal, but by then social services were on their way over. Shortly after she arrived home, a young, thin, white social worker knocked on the door. As usual, all or most of the authority figures I met growing up were white.

The social worker arrived with the police, and my mom quickly told Letiecia and me to sneak into her room and get her weed out of the house while she showed the authorities around the kitchen. Letiecia and I stole a little weed and went to the park to smoke it while we waited for the police to leave. Thank God we had minimal food, or they might have taken us all away. Because of this incident, my mom had to check in with the social worker for several months. I saw how it stressed my mother out and how pissed off she was. In my mind, Joey had caused all of her added troubles, so I was pissed at him too. Life was hard enough as it was, and now the county was on our backs at every turn.

To help me forget all the stuff that was happening at home, I would go out with my friends, all of us around fifteen or sixteen years old. We would get all dressed up and wear our "coochie cutters" and walk for hours down a beautiful two-mile walking trail on Lake Michigan in hopes of picking up guys. There were always some thirsty men there hoping to meet little girls. Without hesitation, us hoochie mommas would go to party with random grown-ass men. That's how I met my son's father.

Walking up the trail on the side of Lake Michigan, we heard loud music bumping. We giggled with excitement hoping the music would lead us to some men. As we walked up the hill into the parkway, I saw a group of black men. Milo Elijah was leaning against his white Corvette parked at one of the stops. The car had 20-inch rims on the front wheels and 22s on the rear, which caused the back of the car to sit up a little bit. As we approached, he was bumping the song "Oh Boy" by Cameron. He and his friends were just chilling, listening to music, and drinking vodka and cranberry juice out of red plastic Solo cups.

"Hey girls, y'all want a drank?" we heard shouted from a well-dressed, sharply groomed man, who was shorter and kind of plump, wearing a huge white-gold and diamond chain.

"Hell yeah, we want some," I replied as we strolled over to the car.

With one glance, I knew I didn't care for Milo. He was short, round, stubby, and had a cute face when he smiled, but he was super arrogant. He compensated for his short stature by talking loudly and being flashy with his diamond rings and multiple gold chains. *Not Milo type*, I thought. Then, I glanced over at his tall, muscular friend Henry, who was much more appealing. He looked like the rapper Ludicrous with tight cornrows going straight down the back of his head.

Henry and Milo were best friends in their early to mid-thirties. I was a fourteen-year-old high school sophomore. In normal society, there should have been no way we were all hanging out there together in the way that we were. But this was Kenosha and at that time, as far as I was concerned Aaliyah had it right, "Age Ain't Nothing But a Number." Milo seemed drawn to me and was highly annoyed that I was looking at Henry.

Milo invited us to go for a ride. Within minutes, he busted out a huge bag of cocaine and asked, "Do you girls play with that white girl?" "On my momma, I was hoping y'all had some!" I excitedly proclaimed. We got lit and then Henry and I hooked up.

After that incident, Henry and I became a thing, even though at the time, I was off and on with Bamm, the guy I had met at Veronica's place. Bamm and I weren't really "official," so hooking up with Henry seemed okay to me. For some reason, Milo was always picking on me and Henry, teasing us, calling Henry a broke ass-nigga and calling me all kinds of names. At the time, I assumed he was just being an asshole. Now I know it was because he wanted me for himself. Henry and I continued dating for a couple of months.

In Kenosha, there were only a few mixed girls like me at the time. One of them was Tamika. She was much prettier than I was, and she had bigger boobs and a perfect booty. I was like a twig-super awkward; she was voluptuous and was always smiling. To this day, she never knew but I was secretly jealous of her. A previous boyfriend had left me for her in middle school, but I never had any hate in my heart for her. I just admired her and felt she was way hotter than I was. Now that I am wise, I know we both express our own unique beauties, and comparison is simply the killer of joy. One day at school, I overheard Tamika describe a guy she was dating. The description sounded exactly like Henry. I interrupted her conversation and confirmed that it was Henry. When I found out she was dating him, I was pissed. *Fuck him,* I thought. On the entire way home, I was pissed. *How could Henry fuck around behind my back like that? Well, at least I still have Bamm.*

At this time, I was living at Veronica's and Bamm stayed there too. That day, when I got home, he was sitting in the living room watching TV and I started cleaning up just to take my mind off Henry. As I was going through some clothes that I was about to wash, I picked up a pair of Bamm's jeans and found a crumpled-up piece of paper inside one of the pockets. It was a love letter to him from a girl he had been dating. She was a girl that he swore was his best friend. He used to say he would never sleep with her because she was so unattractive. *What the fuck? He's cheating on me, too?* Now I was furious, as all the guys I was with were cheating on me too. I didn't want any of them. I yelled at Bamm and told him he wasn't shit, then I kicked him out. The girl who wrote the love letter picked him up.

I was furious and wanted to party to take my mind off Bamm's cheating and Henry's betrayal, so I called Milo. He picked me up in his corvette that night. We went to a club not far away, just over the state line in Illinois. We stopped at his house to grab his Escalade—he really liked showing off and now I know he was trying to save on getting a room. I was only fifteen, but with Milo, that never mattered. Everyone we met would treat him like he was a king. When I saw that, it enticed me because I really liked being with the boss. It made me feel powerful. We hooked up that night in his Escalade. Afterwards, he went to drop me off at Veronica's. By then, it was around three o'clock, and as I opened the door to the apartment, Bamm was there crying.

"Who were you with?" He asked.

I told him, "None of your business. Go be with your fat bitch!"

Bamm grabbed my arms to look me in the face and said, "I don't want that bitch, I want you!" He firmly pressed into my arms and said, "Who the fuck were you with, you little slut?"

I replied, "Fuck you! I was with my new man."

He picked me up and carried me into the house as I kicked and screamed like he was kidnapping me. He grabbed my face and kissed me. The next thing I know he was ripping my clothes off and we had sex. When he finished, he commented on how nasty it was that I was just with Milo. "Don't ever talk to that nigga again," he said, half pleading and half demanding.

A couple weeks later, I was at home on the couch and decided to light a Newport cigarette (I had been smoking since I was ten years old). It tasted horrible, so I put it out instantly and suddenly, I hated the smell of cigarettes. When I went to throw the cigarettes out, the garbage smelled strong, so I took the garbage out and got ready for a party. At the party, I poured a glass of my favorite Southern Comfort and Coke. Within a few moments, I was projectile vomiting everywhere. I knew something was off, so I went home and went to sleep. When I woke up, I could smell the garbage again even though I had just taken the trash out the day before. I knew something was up, but I wasn't sure what until I tried drinking again that evening.

Yep, I vomited again.

"Ewww, nasty!" Veronica said. "Girl, what's wrong with you? How come you suddenly can't hold your liquor?

"I don't know what's wrong," I said.

Then, Veronica gave me a side-eye look and raised her eyebrows. "Girl, I bet you're pregnant."

Oh shit! My mind flashed back to that night with Milo and Bamm. I didn't use a condom with either of them, so I guess it was possible I was pregnant. And now that I thought about it, I hadn't gotten my period. Initially, that didn't bother me because my cycle was kind of irregular anyway, but now the pieces were all falling into place. *Fuck!* I ran to get a pregnancy test and quickly saw the positive result. Fear poured over my entire body. Bamm and I were finally doing well for the first time ever. I feared he would leave once he knew I was pregnant because he knew the chances of my baby being his were small. I had to know right away if he was going to leave me, so I called him, and he came over.

As soon as he arrived, I told him with tears in my eyes that I was pregnant. He hugged me and said, "That's my fucking baby, no matter what." I knew at that point he was with me. I just felt so much shame that he was committed, and we had no idea if the baby was his. Once I felt secure that he wouldn't leave me, I let the idea sink in that I was going to be a mom. In that moment, I decided I would be a better mom to my kid than my mom had been to me. Since I was going to bring a kid into this world, I wanted to give it all the love and attention I could, and I vowed to make a better life for it than what my mom had provided for me. Never mind how I was going to do it; I just knew I would figure it out no matter what. But first, I had to tell my mom.

I knew I couldn't hide the pregnancy for long, so I had to tell my mom quickly. She'd be pissed, for sure, but there wasn't anything she could do. I wasn't going to have an abortion, so she would just have to accept the fact that I was pregnant. Knowing the way her temper worked, I knew the longer I took to tell her, the more pissed she would be. She could be violent at times. All of us kids had been on the worst side of her temper, and it was never pretty. I'd seen her beat Letiecia with a bat and smack Joey so hard he passed out. I was afraid of my mom, so I had to figure out a way to break the news in a way that would prevent her from becoming violent with me. In the meantime, I knew I would need a job, so I applied to several places around town. Within days of finding out I was pregnant, I found a job at a famous Italian deli, Tenuta's. Also, I knew that I would need daycare for school, so I applied to Reuther Central High, which had a program for pregnant students. I was determined to make something of myself.

My mom had a friend called Cece who lived near Veronica. Cece had always been nice to me and my brother and sister. I was terrified of telling my mom I was pregnant, but I felt safer telling Cece and asking her to help me tell my mom. Cece came over to our house one evening with the sole purpose of facilitating a conversation with my mom and me. From my spot on the living room floor, I watched them quietly as they sat on the couch and smoked weed, gossiping about their other friends, and laughing about basic stuff. Then, Cece led into the real reason she was there that night.

"V, your baby is having a baby," she said.

My mom's laughter stopped. She looked towards me, and I could see fire in her eyes. Her chest began to heave up and down as she tried unsuccessfully to control her breathing. Then, she slammed her empty glass down onto the coffee table, stood up, and yelled, "What the fuck is wrong with you? You were supposed to be the one that made something with your life! Now you will never finish school. You'll never be shit!

Get the fuck out! Get all your shit and get outta my house! I'm done with you."

Part of me felt the sting of rejection from my mom's reaction, and part of me was angry. I responded, "You don't know shit. Watch me finish school and be a better mom than you!" I was ballsy and also felt she wouldn't hit me while I was pregnant. My anger fueled my determination to prove her wrong. She yelled a bunch of other stuff at me as I went to my room and gathered the few things I still had there into a garbage bag. I didn't want to live with Veronica and be around all the partying now that I was pregnant. I wanted a healthy life for my baby and Veronica smoked cigarettes and weed like a chimney. I called Bamm and he took me to his grandmother's house. Margaret had a lot of kids and even more grandbabies. She was a lovely Southern woman who made everyone feel loved and cared for. She had a big house, and all those kids and grandkids were living off her. She let Bamm and me take the unfinished basement.

The next day, I was ready for my first job and a new school. From the moment I found out I was pregnant, everything I did was for my kid and to prove my mom wrong about me. Even though she was a huge motivation for me to do better, just to show her I was better than what she thought of me, I was grateful for the fire she lit under me. Once I knew I had a life growing inside of me, I instantly loved it more than I loved myself. I wanted to provide for my child more than anything else in life. With both a note of revenge directed towards my mom, and a deep, unexplainable love for my child, I got busy building my life.

Once I entered the pregnancy program at school, I started to learn about what was happening inside of me and what the baby was experiencing as it grew. I learned that smoking weed, and cigarettes was bad for me and the baby, even though my mom told me she smoked weed and cigarettes throughout her pregnancies. What better example did I need to quit weed? I did it anyways. My body did me a favor by rejecting alcohol and cigarettes from the moment I got pregnant, so that was good. I started learning about nutrition and how to properly nourish myself and my baby. Before then, nutrition was McDonald's for me. McDonalds and Taco bell were seen as luxuries. Once I understood a basic level of nutrition, I incorporated foods that could have a positive impact on my baby.

Still not sure if my baby's daddy was Bam or Milo, I carried this grief and shame in my body my entire pregnancy. A few months in and my health slowly deteriorated. I lost my first job because I would puke all day long and so I couldn't serve food in that state. Instantly, I got two more jobs. Thankfully, my new school and new jobs were all on the same road, which made getting to each of them convenient. At this time, I had no idea how stress affected me or my baby, I was poisoning us both while doing everything I knew for our health.

After a few months, I was hospitalized for a severe kidney and bladder infection. Within a few days I was released from the hospital and was put on bed rest with a catheter. I had overworked myself, and my body was struggling with all kinds of infections. Determined to graduate on time, I felt more upset about missing school than being sick. Knowing I had to complete four years of coursework in two years to graduate on time, pushed me to overwork myself. I went to school in pain with my catheter, against doctors' orders, just to accomplish my goal.

One day at work, I felt massive cramps. I immediately went into a panic. With no transportation of my own, I relied on a coworker to rush me to the hospital's emergency room. I was examined, and I learned that the birth was happening too soon, leading the doctor to chemically stop the birth. This happened two more times. The third time was July third. My baby was due three weeks later. After a few hours of excruciating pain, I started dilating, but it was a slow process. Ten hours later, I was dilated enough to get the epidural. Even after the epidural, I was still slightly dilated.

The day my son was born, I was terrified. Even though this was the third time I had gone into labor, I was scared. I wasn't ready. I didn't know what to expect, and there was no one around who was able to comfort me through the ordeal I was about to endure. After being all alone for hours, my mother came rushing into the hospital room. She looked high on crack and started yelling at the nurses. They kicked her out immediately. Then, Bamm arrived, followed by his aunt. When I saw her, I was embarrassed because I was lying there with my legs open, and my vagina exposed. It was bad enough to have the nurses and techs in and out of the room but having Bamm's aunt see me like that was too much for me. I asked his aunt to leave because of my discomfort.

As soon as she left, a nurse came into the room, put on some gloves, then rubbed some lubricant on her fingers and began to massage my vagina. As she massaged me, she said, "This will help make sure you don't tear." I was riddled with embarrassment in a state of shock. With the snap of the nurse's rubber gloves, I heard the wheels of her rolling stool as she pushed away from the bed before she left the room. No sooner did I exhale and push back up in the bed did my mother came back in.

"Well, look at you," she said. I could tell immediately that she was amped up but was not as high as before. "How ya doing?" she asked.

"I'm in pain and this epidural isn't helping."

"What the fuck?" my mom screamed. "Somebody better get up in here and help my baby. She's hurting."

As the pain of the contractions increased, the nurse told me the doctor would be there shortly. The anesthesiologist then gave me something that numbed my entire body, allowing me to rest pain-free for two hours. As the medication was wearing off, the doctor was still not there, and the nurse told me I couldn't have more because I would need to use my muscles to push during the delivery. By the time the doctor finally arrived, I had been in full-blown labor for over fourteen hours. After hours of pushing, I begged the doctor to pull the baby out of me because he was kicking his feet through my ribs. Using forceps to guide the baby through the birth canal, the doctor tugged and twisted for what seemed like an hour. The pain was agonizing, and I was sure I would pass out at any moment.

Finally, at 4:19 p.m. on July 4th, Mauriion Lavell Price was born. From his first breath, he began crying softly. His cry sounded like a cat's meow, which I thought was divine, almost angelic. Everyone else in the delivery room, however, seemed super scared. His Apgar score—measuring of a newborn's appearance, pulse, grimace, activity, and respiration—was extremely low, and I noticed the fear on the faces of the doctor and nurses. Something was seriously wrong, but they didn't know what. The doctor wanted a geneticist to see Mauriion immediately.

"You need to sign off allowing the ambulance to take him to Children's Hospital in Milwaukee," the nurse said. "You have a severe bacterial infection in your uterus, so you need to stay here to recover."

There was no way I was going to allow them to take my baby from me. "Hell no, are you kidding? If he goes, I go," I screamed, in agony and pure determination.

If I had to, I would get up and walk out of there on my own two feet, but I wasn't about to let them rush my baby to another hospital while I stayed there waiting to find out what happened. Instead, I signed a waiver indicating that if I died, the hospital could not be held liable for allowing me to leave. I rode in the ambulance with my son, scared to death, not knowing if he was going to make it. I was in so much physical pain from birth and the infection in my uterus, but there was nothing that would keep me from my baby.

Once we arrived at Children's Hospital, we were assigned a room where I could breastfeed my baby. The nurses were in and out at all times of the day. Sometimes they took him away to run tests on him, which had me in a panic, afraid they wouldn't bring him back or they would harm him in some way. No one was there with me—not my mother, or Joey or Letiecia—and no one explained what all the tests were for. Bamm popped in here and there and I refused to leave my baby alone. For what seemed like forever, I was laid up in the hospital going in and out of consciousness, healing from the infection, recovering from the fatigue of birth, and hoping for the best for my son.

When the doctors came in, they told me the tests revealed that Mauriion had some kind of chromosomal disorder, but they didn't know which one. They wanted me to be prepared because some of these disorders result in death for the babies pretty quickly.

"No, he's not dying. He's gonna be fine," I said.

There was no way I could lose my baby. He was the only thing that kept me wanting to be alive at that point. My family didn't want me. His daddy was unreliable. My entire life was hellish . . . except for my son. I needed him to live so I could live.

That night, I cried to sleep and prayed for a miracle.

A few days later, the nurse came to my room with a wheelchair and took me to a small meeting room in the hospital. There were about five doctors in the room seated at a conference table. And then there was me. It was beyond intimidating. The white coats told me that my son was missing a piece of his fifth chromosome. This disorder was called Cri Du Chat Syndrome. They went through all this medical talk with still emotionless faces to explain all the common complications that come with Cri Du Chat. They suggested putting a permanent feeding tube in him. Getting him to breastfeed was nearly impossible because he wouldn't latch on to my boob, and when he did, he wasn't drinking much because he would become so tired from trying to suckle. They said his chances of latching on were slim to none.

The doctor continued: "A lot of these kids have very low muscle tone and many die very young, in their teen years. If they make it to their thirties, they die from aspiration."

That was not what I wanted to hear. There I was at sixteen, faced with the possibility that my son might not make it to his teens. I thought by having my son, I would always have someone to love. I was scared and angry, but I still had a fire in my belly.

"That's just a book," I said. "If you put a hole in his stomach won't that make his muscles weaker? No, you're not gonna put a feeding tube in him. You can't tell me what my son is going to do or who he's going to be. He's going to do everything he needs to do in his own time. He's going to learn everything in his own time. He's gonna be fine."

I decided at that point that I was going to love him and treat him like a regular kid. By then, I was tired of the word "normal" and decided to discard it from my vocabulary. My will to be the best I could be from the moment he was born was overwhelming. Of course, I unconsciously wavered throughout my life but consciously I did everything I could to be the best parent. Even though I didn't know what his best was, my desire was to do everything I could to make sure he had a good life. I refused the feeding tube because putting a permanent hole in his stomach was a sure way to discourage him from ever eating on his own. I also believed a hole in his stomach would make it harder for him to walk. He would be forever dependent on that thing to do something I was sure he could do by himself.

About a month and a half later, Mauriion was still in the NICU lab and still wasn't drinking enough. The hospital decided to exercise their legal right to do the surgery for the feeding tube, so they scheduled the surgery without my consent. When I found out, I was so pissed. Thankfully, they told me the surgery was scheduled for the following day. All I could do was pray for a miracle. "God, please help. This can't be what's supposed to happen to my precious little baby."

The night before the surgery, a little bit after midnight, Mauriion woke up with his angelic cry. I picked him up and he started moving his lips and mouth, so I fed him. I rubbed his little back and sang to him as he ate. As if on cue, he started suckling and he didn't stop. He drank two milliliters over the required amount, just enough so they could not do the surgery the next day. My prayers had been answered. It was a miracle. I knew it was God's work! A few days later, my son was released from the hospital. I had fought for him and won. I felt victorious as this was the first time I consciously listened to my intuition, and it worked!

Throughout the entire ordeal, I was spiritually supported yet physically all alone. Everyone in my family was on drugs, partying, and didn't seem to care. Bamm was in and out for visits in between all the parties he was going to, having sex with all kinds of other people while I was stuck in the hospital in pain fighting for my baby's life. He'd stop in for a few minutes, but I soon realized he didn't care about me. My sister had been in and out of hospitals and had a beautiful baby girl 3 weeks after me. My brother, who was a runaway at the time, didn't take my calls because he thought I was trying to set him up. Months earlier, he had done some really mean stuff to my mom, which pissed me off. As a result, we had a big argument and I said he wasn't my brother anymore, so he still didn't trust me.

After I left the hospital, I went back to my apartment, two jobs, and school. My best friend at the time, Kim, helped me with babysitting while I worked as many shifts as I could get so I could make some money to feed us. I would wake up, take the bus to school, walk to her place to drop off my kid, and then walk to one job, be there for four hours, walk to the other job, then pick up my kid, and go home. This was my life. I could only hope life would get better, but I had no indication that it would. All I had was my son and a heart full of hope that my life would improve.

That was enough.

When Mauriion drank the milk that night, that was the inspiration I needed to believe he would be okay for the rest of his life. I choose to see it as a sign. There was no rhyme or reason for me to know this; I just couldn't bear to believe what the doctors said. That was divine inspiration before I knew what that was.

What I learned over many experiences throughout my life is that when I decide something, the universe conspires to make that decision a reality. Everyone has access to that divine support. All it takes is to first decide what you want. Trust in the process and take actions towards what you are guided to. You have the free will to choose, and that is powerful.

After Mauriion was born, I continued messing with Milo. One ordinary day we were driving around drinking and partying, along with my best friend's sister, Angela. Milo declared, "We should have a threesome."

My inner reaction was immediate: *Hell no!* But what I said was, "No, I am good."

Abruptly, he pulled into a dark alley and threatened me. "Theresa, who the fuck do you think you are to tell me no? Bitch I own you! Tell me no again and you will end up in this dumpster dead." By the way he spoke, and the furious look in his eyes, I knew he was serious. "Angela, are you gonna say anything if I kill her right now?"

Angela's eyes bugged out as she shook her head, and gave a quiet, "Nope."

In the eerie silence that followed, I felt helpless. *You know he's crazy enough to do it*, my mind warned. He always had a gun on him, so I was afraid of him, but I was also drawn to his power. Part of me knew the danger I was in, but I thought I deserved it. I had grown to have love for him, but I don't think I was ever in love with him. That power he embraced turned me on, and I was attracted to it, I think because I didn't know my own power. After that incident, we kept messing around and I got pregnant with twins. They were due on my eighteenth birthday.

By then, I was still close to Bamm's family. When his mom found out I was pregnant again, she warned me: "You got to get an abortion, Theresa. You can't do three kids. What if they all have disabilities? There's no way you're going to be able to survive."

Yet again, I had no idea who the father was. It could have been Milo's or Bamm's, as they were the main guys I messed around with. I never liked being alone, so I had a bunch of side niggas.

One night, Milo came over to my apartment and threatened me, saying, "You're not fucking having these kids." We argued. He yelled at me: "Get over here! I'm gonna fucking punch you in your stomach. I'll kill em for free!"

He chased me around outside of the apartment, but he was short, and fat and I was able to get away. For days, Bamm's mother's words rang in my ears. Maybe she was right; maybe all my kids would be born with problems. How could I take care of them all? Besides that, I didn't want to bring two more kids into this fucked-up world, especially since all possible dads were crazy, and so was I. As a young kid, I was against abortion. With all the fear, I ended up having an abortion. That was another devastating decision.

When I woke up in a bed after the abortion, I cried uncontrollably. Nothing and no one could calm me, so I just cried and cried; so much so that they kicked me out because I was disturbing the other patients. Still heavily sedated, Milo helped me to the car, and I slumped over once inside because I couldn't hold myself up physically. When I woke up, I felt the strongest sense of self-hate I'd ever had. I truly was disgusted with myself. If I didn't have Mauriion to care for, I would have killed myself for sure. That's how much I hated myself.

When Milo dropped me off in front of my apartment complex, he didn't even bother to walk me up to my place. He was so annoyed with all my crying that he just wanted to leave. That really pissed me off. Despite being mad at Milo, I was just so tired and miserable and ashamed that I went straight to my bedroom and went to sleep. When I woke up hours later, I had the most excruciating stomach cramps ever. Shooting pains all throughout my body made me sure it was from the abortion. I believed I was being punished because I shouldn't have killed my babies. As I lay there in pain, a friend called to check on me. I could barely breathe let alone talk. She rushed over and took my temperature. It was 104. We rushed to the hospital.

The abortion nearly killed me. I got very sick, and I almost died.

A part of one of the babies was left inside me, which caused an infection and severe fever. Even in the hospital, while shivering in the ice bath as the doctors tried to get my fever down, Milo was there in the room, drunk, and laughing at the whole scene, saying, "You should have just let me take care of it." Of course, that wasn't funny, but at least Milo paid for the abortion and took me to the clinic. I didn't have a car and was living off a $5 per hour salary.

While I was screwing around and getting pregnant by other men, Bamm got my friend pregnant and gave her my engagement ring, so I cut him off permanently. He became violent at that point and started climbing up to the balcony of my second-story apartment, stealing my kid, and choking me. At one point, I came home, and he had busted out the lights along the stairway up to my apartment. As I walked up the stairs, he jumped, hiding in the dark hall and attacked me. Thankfully, I maneuvered and kicked him down the stairs, then ran inside and tried to lock the door, but he got in. He pushed through the door and then took my kid and ran off. I called the cops and when they arrived, they arrested me for some warrant for an unpaid speeding ticket. I was taken to jail and had to pay a fine, but nothing happened to Bamm. He was going to school to be a police officer, so they didn't want to arrest one of their own, no matter how crazy he was.

Despite his crazy behavior, I always found it shocking how well Bamm's family treated me. His grandmother was one of the first people who didn't ask me for anything, and she never made me feel ashamed or low. She just loved me. After that incident, she told me to keep some grits on the stove so that if Bamm ever climbed the balcony again, I could pour it on him, burn him, and he would stop really quick. By then, I had done the blood test that said Mauriion was not Bamm's. Neither Bamm, nor anyone in his family believed the blood test because Mauriion looked just like Bamm and nothing like Milo. The blood test showed that Bamm was one marker away from being the father. So I had Milo give samples too, and his test was conclusive; the baby was Milo's. That's when Milo told me he was married.

"What the hell? You're out every night with 15-, 16-, and 17-year-old girls! How does that work?"

The confusing part was that he was married to the principal of a school.

What the fuck? He also told me he already had ten kids. I only knew about one.

"I'm over here struggling," I said, "and you're over there living it up and laughing as you pass me in the streets with your kid?"

Disgusted, I decided to put him on child support as soon as I turned eighteen. I waited until I was of age because I wanted support and didn't want him to go to jail.

Everything in my life has been a choice, good and bad. I chose to hook up with the guys I hooked up with. I chose to smoke weed and get drunk. I also chose to graduate on time with no evidence of my ability to do that, and to be the best mother I could be to my son. Everything is a choice. Our choices and beliefs either motivate or demotivate our actions. Over time, I have applied this truth to my life in many circumstances, and as a result, nearly everything I believed would happen has happened.

If you were exactly where you wanted to be, you really wouldn't have any purpose. Your purpose is to expand and to create. Without that, you just live, eat, work, and sleep. For some that is a redundant life, for others it is a perfect life. Follow your guidance, learn to trust your heart, and everything will work out eventually.

COMPASSION FOR MY MOM AND FINDING MY DAD

Looking back at the amount of abandonment and rejection my mother felt from her parents, I understand why she was how she was. At a very young age, I realized that my mother's choices in men were horrible. My dad was a rapist (or so I thought). Letiecia's dad was a rapist, murderer and gangster, and Joey's dad was a raging, violent, abusive, scary man. I vowed early on to never date the kind of men my mother did.

This is why it is so important to share the good, the bad, and most importantly, the ugly with your children. It starts with digging deep within the wounds that shaped your life. Then, you need to forgive all parties, especially yourself, for all that happened along the way. Forgiveness is the key to releasing the trapped emotions from your body and, therefore preventing that energy from holding you back in life. Stuck energy is the root of dis-ease. Donna Eden is a powerful teacher of Energy Medicine. She works with judges, doctors and all kinds of incredible people because she can help heal from anger and a myriad of medical diseases with simple quick movements. She is always saying, "Where energy flows, healing goes". Her work saved me from depression, anxiety and helped me cultivate joy with a few simple movements she calls "Daily Energy Medicine." She has affordable courses and so much free information on YouTube. I bet many of the world's problems would be solved in less than a decade if everyone was forgiving daily and doing daily energy medicine. I wonder how much joy, love and forgiveness could be created if we practiced forgiveness as a family? How cool would it be to normalize it in each household? I talk about a lot of the negative habits learned because that is what I learned. My hope is that you investigate your own habits and create space for more healthy uplifting habits. The more we move our bodies the more energy we have flowing. The quicker we forgive, the less judgmental we are, and that allows more guidance, support, and love into your mind, body, and soul.

Speaking of unhealthy habits, the only time I really thought I might lose my mom was a few weeks before my twentieth birthday. My mom told me she was going to kill herself because she was "tired of every-fucking thing."

I said, "You're the only thing I have in the world. Please don't leave me."

Then, she suddenly blurted out, "Your dad's name is Charles Brownley."

That was the first time I'd heard his name. She told me what really happened and admitted that she had lied all those years ago about being raped by a military guy. The truth was that she had been a prostitute. She was so ashamed about her life back then that she didn't want anyone to know the real story.

When she told me the truth, the whole story, part of me was so angry that she had lied to me all those years. I hated her for keeping the truth from me; for making me believe a lie, and a terrible one at that; for allowing our entire family to hate me for something that wasn't even my fault; for being who she was back then and bringing me into this world. I felt alone and I wondered if my real dad even knew I existed.

She had no idea where to find him or even if he was still alive.

That's when I got the idea of finding him. For months, I searched for Charles Brownley, based on the little information my mom provided. I went online and looked through ancestry websites, directories, and even social media. Finally, I found my dad right before my mom died. He was living in Sheboygan, Wisconsin when I found him, less than two hours from where I grew up.

From the moment I first saw Charles—his face, his eyes, and his nose—I felt like I was at home. I knew he was my dad. And my heart melted when he claimed me immediately. When he looked at me, he said, "Yeah, I really believe you're my daughter because we have the same nose and you have a very loving heart, just like me." He then said, "I always thought you were mine, but your mom said you weren't. Then Joey's dad said that if he ever came around again, he would kill me and you all."

Charles told me he had been in love with my mom all those years ago. He had won the lottery and thought that if he gave her everything she wanted, she would be with him. Then, she got pregnant. Back then, she was with José, my brother Joey's dad, who told Charles that if he ever came back to Kenosha, José would kill him, my mom, and all of us. Charles was terrified. Knowing that my mom was a prostitute, he didn't even know if I was really his kid. So, instead of fighting for her and for me, he just went about his life.

I wanted to do the DNA test, but I didn't get the blood test right away. As the weeks went by, we would talk for hours at a time. He was so caring. His voice was so soothing, and he seemed to never get tired of talking to me. I felt his love in every conversation.

My father, Charles Brownley was a lawyer, and he had many academic degrees. By then, his days were filled with caring for his girlfriend, who was severely disabled. She had a stroke and had the mentality of a 5-year-old after that. He was taking courses for his own personal satisfaction. One time, I went to his house to pick him up so we could go out to dinner. When his girlfriend saw me, she had a fit. She obviously had the wrong idea, thinking there was something between us other than a father/ daughter relationship. I apologized to her, and we decided not to go out again.

Eventually, I lost contact with him because I lost my phone and all my phone numbers, including his. I tried searching for my dad with no luck. Several years later, I did the DNA test through 23andMe, and it confirmed that he was my dad. Sadly, he had already died two years before.

In the years following, when I found my cousins on that side of the family using the DNA research, I discovered that his family is also racist. All the mixed kids from both my mom's family and my dad's family were given away. I do not believe I have any siblings on my father's side, but all of the cousins who were mixed were given up for adoption or grew up in foster homes. In 2022, I found a mixed cousin on my mother's side who was abandoned by the family as a baby. The sadness I felt when I discovered that it was only the mixed kids that were given up was unbelievable. But I'm still glad I had the guidance to find and connect with my dad before he died. That meant so much to me, particularly at that time when my mom was dying.

4. THE DARK SIDE

When I turned eighteen, the dark side came in. My high school friend Reana threw me an eighteenth birthday party and invited a bunch of our friends. It was a crazy scene, with lots of drinking and smoking weed. Just as the party got going, Reana pulled me away from the action and took me upstairs to the bathroom. There we were, all alone in this quiet room, but I could still hear the pumping of the music from downstairs.

"I got something for you," she said.

I thought it was going to be coke, but the next thing I knew she grabbed me around the waist, then pulled me closer to her. And then she kissed me on the lips. A deep, wet, luscious kiss that had my head spinning. The next thing I knew, she pulled down my pants and guided me to the jacuzzi ledger and went down on me. I loved it. It had never been this intense. Before that night, we would make out and finger each other, but we didn't go down on each other. This was nothing new for me. I played with nearly every best friend I had as a kid. We always kept it in the dark and never spoke of it again. That night was the start of a secret affair between Reana and me.

The next day, we decided to visit a sex shop to pick up toys for our little escapades. She drove us to Illinois right across the border because we didn't want our secret to get out. We were all excited to go into the store because it was connected to a strip club. After picking up a few toys, we went inside the club. At the door was a big, tall, burly guy with a long white beard and dark glasses.

We said, "Hi, how much to get in?"

He said, "Uh, no, I don't think so. You must be with a guy to get in here."

Reana and I looked at each other with surprise. I said, "That's discrimination."

He laughed, then looked us both up and down like we were a couple of kids coming to start trouble.

"Nope," he said. "You're either trying to steal our customers or fight our girls if you're coming in here by yourself. We ain't having none of that shit. Go home."

We walked outside pissed off, kicking rocks and cursing. Just then, two guys walked up and started talking to us.

"What's up girls? What are you doing out here?"

Reana said, "Well, we were trying to get into the club, but the bouncer said we couldn't come in without a guy."

I halfway thought they would walk us in, pretending to be our dates. Instead, they offered us a job. Turns out those two were the owner and the DJ at the strip club.

"He's right," the one guy said. "You can't just go in there as a customer looking like you look, all sexy and shit. But you can work here. Some girls make a thousand bucks a night."

When he said that number, my mouth dropped open, and all kinds of thoughts ran through my mind. *What the hell? I'm making just over five bucks an hour at both of my jobs. This is way better.*

"Well, let us go onstage together because I'm not going up there by myself," I said.

"I'm too afraid." I was scared, but eager to start making some real money.

He agreed and Reana was with it, so we were in. We went next door to get something cute to wear and went back. As soon as we got inside, we realized it was a fully nude club. One of the strippers escorted us to the back, where we got undressed, picked out a few props to take with us onstage, freshened up our hair and makeup, then trotted out there to see what we could do.

We downed a bottle of Malibu hiding in the corner.

"Are you ready for this?" Reana asked me. I could tell she was kind of scared. So was I but we had gone this far, so we might as well go all the way.

"I'm as ready as I'll ever be," I said. "Let's do it!"

Fifteen minutes later we had made a hundred bucks on one song. That night, I made four hundred dollars. That was more than I made in two weeks from both of my fast-food jobs. I was hooked. Instead of quitting my gigs at Wendy's and Dairy Queen, I kept those jobs during the day and worked at the strip club at night. My plan was to only strip for a little while so I could get a car because I had been taking the bus to the hospital with Mauriion whenever he got sick. I was doing cocaine and Adderall and drinking, then going to the next job hungover and barely functioning. Eventually, I quit Wendy's and was fired from Dairy Queen because I was late after being up all night. My life had turned upside down fast, and I wasn't ready to go back to the way things were. Once I got fired from Dairy Queen, working at the strip club became way more fun because I had more energy. I wasn't so tired from running around.

None of my family knew what I was doing to make money. They all thought I still worked fast food. But then, my mom found out. One day while she was over at my house, she came across my gym bag.

"What's all this stuff in here? Where are you going?" she asked.

She pulled out one item after another from my bag: panties, 9-inch shiny stripper heals, deodorant, makeup, and baby wipes. As soon as she saw the baby wipes, she flipped. She badgered me thinking I was hooking. But really, I used the wipes to freshen up between sets at the club because there were no showers. Even though the money was good, I felt so ashamed of working at that club. There was no way I could have slept with men for money at that point. I simply didn't have the courage. When she didn't believe me, it deeply hurt my heart. *How could my own mother think I was a prostitute?* When I told her that I was stripping and where, she was pissed.

"I know what they do at that club and it ain't dancing. What the fuck is wrong with you?" she said.

As it turned out, that was the same club where my mom worked right before she started prostituting. I had no idea. She did not explain how she knew the club.

Working at the club was like every girl for herself. I came in like a storm and I made so much money that the other strippers hated me. There was so much hate and jealousy and greed there. My life was threatened several times. One of the girls poured rubbing alcohol into my Caribbean Malibu rum. That scared the shit out of me because I could have been killed. When I finally got a car—one of those big-body old school Chevys—someone poked holes in my brake lines. When I drove away that night, I ran into the side of a snowbank. Thank God the snowbank was there. All of this was in the hands of the other strippers. It was petty, but it showed me who they were. I made some friends but made even more enemies.

My stage name quickly turned into an avatar and became Tianna. I had a friend in high school, a beautiful white girl with parents who loved and spoiled her. I admired and I wished I had her life, so I chose her name. I always wanted to be a white girl, for some reason. Probably because my mom was white. Tianna was like my hidden shadow, my alter ego, who emerged from my depths whenever I stripped. I didn't identify as a stripper when I was outside of the club, only when I was there as Tianna. It was probably a safety mechanism to keep me from feeling shame and guilt all the time.

I felt like a lame stripper until I learned the pole. I stayed late to practice every night until I could work it, which didn't take too long. I'm a fast learner and I started doing flips on that pole, plus all kinds of crazy stuff. I had no fear, so I just went for it and got better and better. Everyone noticed. My first DJ once told me, "Wow girl, look at you. When you first started, you looked like a monkey trying to climb up that pole you'd just slide right off". With the extra attention and compliments, I began coming in early to amplify my progression. I didn't realize it at the time, but that demonstrated my work ethic and commitment.

People don't often think about work ethic in this way, but that's exactly what it was. First of all, I had three jobs. Then, I made the decision to go with the money. That's self-preservation and survival and providing for my child. I figured out the game quickly. In a club, there are a hundred guys. Only a couple are going to say yes, so it's a numbers game. I took every no as a next. Not being their cup of tea was nothing to cry over. Some of the girls would go and have to smoke and get drunk, do a couple shots really quick after a rejection before they could get the courage to go to the next one. Not me. I didn't have time for that. I just kept going.

My brother moved in with me a few months after I started stripping. I had been paying babysitters to watch Mauriion while I worked, so it was nice to have my brother there to care for my son. Joey was so sweet and patient with Mauriion, and that comforted me knowing my kid was well cared for when I wasn't around. Joey also had a lot of girls who loved my son. My brother spent his days watching my son and keeping the house clean. I would come home and throw cash at him depending on how much I made and how clean the house was. At first, this was awesome. Joey really catered to me, and that felt great. I took care of all his financial needs, mainly weed, cigarettes, food, and shelter. Having him there gave me a lot of freedom to work and play.

Milo would come by the strip club and make it rain like a thunderstorm. He'd throw a thousand bucks on the stage while I was up there, and people were amazed. They had never seen that. It would hype up the other guys and they would try to match it, so I made a lot of money onstage.

Even while working at the strip club, I kept my thoughts focused on doing better for myself and my son most of the time, even though I regularly let loose and would wild out and party for a week or two here and there. I remembered what I'd thought about in the hospital the night Mauriion was born. I promised myself that I'd be a better mother to him than my mom was to me. To get there, I had to create some better opportunities for myself. That started with me going to college. In my heart, I wanted to help pregnant teenage girls, but I didn't know how.

I enrolled in Gateway Technical College. Thankfully, Joey was my caretaker for Mauriion, so I could focus on school. It didn't take long for me to realize I was out of my league there. I had too much going on in my life to concentrate and give my classwork the attention it deserved. After my first semester, I failed a couple classes, then I dropped out. It was depressing and I felt like a failure. Looking back, I realized the timing was off. I wasn't ready for college. My mind was still in the streets, so instead of feeling sorry for myself, I went heavy into the strip club world.

Around this time, I was being stalked by two Kenosha police. I was terrified and wanted to get out of Kenosha. The cops first pulled me over, without a license, and asked me who my boyfriend was. Then they let me go without giving me a ticket. Two days later, they showed up at the strip club. They sat right in front of the stage but didn't get any dances. About a week later, I went to school and got a call within an hour after leaving home. The same cops had kicked open my door, went into my room, rummaged through my things, and threw my weed and panties that were on my dresser, onto the floor. They must have watched me leave and went in as soon as I did. My brother woke up to them up in the house without a warrant. Right away, I moved to a new home in Kenosha, as if they couldn't find me.

The money had started to dry up because there were fewer customers coming into the strip club. One of the girls I was working with had a side gig at another club in Milwaukee, about an hour away, that was much bigger and nicer than the one I worked at. I decided to drive to Milwaukee to check out this new club and see if I could get in as a dancer. I auditioned on stage in front of a pale overweight white man with dark hair. I danced to one song, got my clothes on, and was told by the front desk that I had been rejected. That made me feel ugly as fuck. I went back to my regular club and started thinking about what else I could do to earn more and get out of Kenosha. The cops kept circling me and I couldn't fathom what they wanted. I figured it must be sexual because I wasn't doing anything crazy, and they literally let me break the law driving without a license and having weed.

A few months later, I had dropped over 15 pounds after having stopped drinking soda. So, I went back to that club in Milwaukee and was hired. Once I saw this beautiful high-end club, I deeply hated working at the crappy club I'd been at. As soon as I was hired, I began to take notice of the owner. He was a tall, handsome white man with piercing blue eyes and a bald head. He dressed in sharp, colorful high-end suits and he smelled delicious. His name was Richard, and he would come in daily and sit in the back in the dark while meeting with some interesting looking characters. It didn't take much for me to realize Richard was a gangster. When I figured it out, I was terrified of him, but for some reason it turned me on. So, I started trying to go out with him. Every time I approached him, he shut me down.

"Listen, if I can't have a drink with you, I'm not messing with you," he said. "Come back when you're twenty-one, kid." That only made me want him more.

Months later, as soon as I turned twenty, I went up to Richard and said, "I'm twenty-one now." He knew right away what I wanted. We had a drink and then we went to his secret hideaway, an apartment not far from the strip club that was secluded. In no time, we were all over each other, pulling each other's clothes off, kissing, and rolling around like two newlyweds. He was a very passionate lover, and his skills blew my mind. I had never been with someone like him. The problem was, Richard was married. Even though I knew about his wife, my hope was that he would leave her and be with me. He joked about leaving her, but he loved her more and simply used me like a toy.

I had never pushed myself on someone as much as I did with Richard. I was really into him. As time went on, we had the most intense exciting relationship ever. He was the most passionate attentive lover I'd ever had. Not surprisingly, I craved him and if anyone got close to him, I got vicious. My attraction to him was centered on a combination of his power, his passion, and how he took care of me and protected me. I felt powerful next to him. When we first started our relationship, the girls at the club were savage. They hated me because they saw what was happening and they were threatened by the possibility that I could have some influence over him and how things were run at the club. As a result, I got into a lot of fights and there were lots of threats against me. None of it phased me though. I was up to the task because I was going after what I wanted. For the first time in my life, I felt safe and cared for. If anyone got too close or disrespectful, he fired or suspended them. This made me feel even more powerful and created a lot of isolation because girls started being afraid of being my friend.

Richard would call me his baby girl, and he took really good care of me. Suddenly, no one fucked with me anymore. At the drop of a hat, I knew I could get any of those girls fired, so they backed off. I was the one in power and everyone knew it. Richard made sure I had vehicles, drivers so I could drink and do anything I needed. He also taught me self-discipline and mental control. He helped me see how my emotions controlled me. As soon as I got upset, all I could do was stew in whatever drama it was. He would say, "Come on kid, one day you will learn to let shit roll off your back." I would think, *if this badass thinks it's no big deal, of course I can let it go.* Because I had been in survival mode my whole life, it was only natural for me to take everything personally. I'd become hyper-sensitive to everything. Every little thing was a big ordeal in my head.

Knowing that Richard saw something special in me helped build my confidence tremendously. In the beginning, I had no confidence; I was faking it. Ironically, most people saw me as confident. They thought I was so calm and in control, but I wasn't I was always scared and always high on multiple things. I didn't feel pretty. I always felt ugly, like something was wrong with me. I saw beauty in everyone else, but never in myself. Being with Richard gave me the courage to believe there was something special about me. He would revel at the way I thought and how I spoke would tell me I was not normal and assured me I would be someone someday. He told me I could be anything I wanted to be. He took me out to fancy places and at times, he valued my opinion. No one else had done that before. His vision of me lit a spark inside of me, his personal story helped me realize that anyone can be successful.

When I decided to go to college, he fully supported me, until he found out what college I was attending and what I was studying. I was accepted into Alverno College, an all-girls Catholic school. When he discovered that, he was pissed off as he said, "You need to study business. And why the fuck do you want to go to a dike school anyway? Are you a fucking dike?"

It was a stupid question that I refused to answer. He probably asked me it 1000 times over the 4 years I attended college. When I started college, things turned ugly. Richard started yelling at me and calling me names in front of the other girls. His first wife went to the same college and left him possibly for another woman, so he was triggered. It was like he wanted to take me down a notch; to lower the confidence he helped me build. He would even push me around in front of the bartenders and bouncers, just because he was mad, and he could. That was about the extent of his physical abuse, yet verbal abuse was frequent and that led to mental and emotional abuse.

For all the good Richard did for me, there were times when he was a vicious animal. Whenever he got mad, everyone ran. He would call people names and yell at anyone in his sight. Most people were rightfully afraid of him. No one spoke with even a hint of attitude to him, but sometimes I'd get ballsy with him when he was rough with me, cursing at him. That only frustrated him more and he would call me a ballsy bitch. When he would get mad at me, he'd fire, then rehire me. That happened multiple times. The whole thing became a sick, ruthless game we would continue to play out.

Richard had a profound sense of superiority because he had built so much success with his businesses. Everyone around him kissed his ass so hard because of his stature and his bold personality. In the same way he could cut people down with his temper and insulting words, he would also be the best supporter anyone could ask for. If he believed in you, he would help you. Many people came to him with a dream, and he helped them financially, with connections, and advice. Other times, he opted to stay out of other people's drama and let them figure it out for themselves. One of those times was when I tried to help a girl who I knew was in deep trouble.

One summer night around 8:30, I arrived at the strip club ready to go. As soon as I got into the back room, I saw a beautiful young black beauty getting ready. She was super friendly and had a huge smile as she introduced herself.

"Hi, I am McKayla, and you are beautiful," she said.

"Awe, thanks hot stuff. You must be new." I replied.

"Yeah, this is my first day. This club is so nice," she said. "I've danced before, but that club was a hole in the wall compared to here."

"Girl, I felt the same way about this place when I started here about a year ago. You'll get used to it and you'll make a lot of money. It gets lit in here!" I smiled; she laughed. "Do you want to do a lap with me?" I asked. "I'll get your first drink." I never paid for drinks because I was always on Richard's tab. But I was being extra because I could.

"Yes please!" she said.

We went to the main floor, and both did a double shot of Crown Royal, then began scouting the club for our next sponsor. I spotted a man named Paul who had spent money on me before, so I knew he was good for at least a room with both of us. "Well hello Tiana. Who is your friend here?" Paul asked.

"This is McKayla, and she is my new naughty friend," I said with a wink.

That's all it took. We sat down and sandwiched Paul, giving him a load of attention. He smiled and giggled as we talked about all the dirty things we wished we could do with him. Within an hour we were in VIP with Paul, and he spent

$700 for every thirty minutes with us. We had fun making money off Paul for nearly two hours. McKayla and I were a powerful team, and we became instant besties.

Within a couple of weeks, I noticed that she seemed really stressed. When we first met, she walked like an ebony queen, but suddenly, she started looking weak and sickly. When I asked what was wrong, she said she was stressed. Then, I saw a huge bruise on her leg and decided to press her for the truth. I could tell she was scared because she refused to talk about it. Finally, one night she went out partying with me and we did coke. That is when she told me she was involved with a guy who was beating her, taking her money, and threatening to hurt her and her family if she left him. She loved and trusted me and was too scared to speak his name, so I never knew who he was. We planned to help her slowly move out. I loved this girl. I always fell in love hard and quick with people, but pulled my love with a fierce, dramatic coldness as soon as I got hurt.

At this point, McKayla and I agreed on everything, and she was the first friend I helped make money who returned the favor and brought me in on her deals as well. Our plan was for her to go back to her apartment and take only a few personal items, along with her dog. That way, her abusive boyfriend wouldn't be suspicious. She never told me who this boyfriend was, so I had no fear of him, and I never saw him. She lied to him and said she was tired of the dog and wanted to get rid of it. He believed in her. Once the dog was out, she was able to move away from him. Once she was out on her own, she told me to watch my back and make sure I wasn't followed whenever I left the club. I already did that because I had been followed out of the club and chased by a stalker once.

A couple of years later, I found out who this man was. One evening, I was walking back to the strip club with a box of pizza after my break. This beautiful young stripper was standing in the back of the building alone. She was about eighteen years old and new at the club. When she first arrived, she was gorgeous, but like McKayla, soon she began to look thin and pale. As I passed her that night, she looked at my pizza and started scanning the back area nervously in search of other people.

Then, she whispered, "Please give me a piece of your pizza before someone comes."

I gave her the entire pizza and asked, "Who are you afraid to eat in front of?"

As it turned out, she was being pimped by a guy, and he had other girls who worked at the club watching out to make sure this girl didn't get friendly with anyone and blow their game. "Please, just walk away if anyone comes while we're talking," she said.

Apparently, none of the pimp's girls were allowed to converse or be friendly with me. She was being punished for speaking to me from time to time. They were starving her until she got in line with the pimp's commands. She knew I helped another girl escape, and she wanted my help. She explained that more than twenty-five girls who worked at the club were owned by this dude, who had hundreds of girls in other states working for him. I was outraged.

I ran to tell Richard, and he said, "What the fuck are you getting involved for? It's none of your business."

Of course, I was pissed at his response, but I wasn't surprised. He had his own business to worry about.

Whether that girl made a run for it or not I never found out, but I do know that the guy found out I was snooping around and said he would kill me if I kept it up. He even came up to the club with a gun one night looking for me. I had friends in high places who protected me, so I thank God nothing happened, but the weird thing is that this was the same guy I had dated for about a week right before I met McKayla. It turned out to be her crazy boyfriend. When I dated him for about a week, he acted like a regular dude and dressed like a thug. We hooked up once. The next morning, he said he had to go collect some money from one of "his girls." I stopped seeing him after that, and I had no idea who he was until this girl spoke his name. That whole incident made me realize that I could have been killed by a crazy pimp. For some reason, God saved me from that.

The dream I have had of having a happy, healthy family someday stopped me from getting involved with over three known pimps. There are many girls working in strip clubs who are being pimped out by guys they think are their boyfriends. If you are one of these girls, please know that a beautiful life is possible once you release the chains of your enslavement. I trust you are on this path for a reason and for however many seasons you choose. If you are with a vicious man, your choice is harder because it very well might be a choice of freedom or death. I believe with God's help you will survive. None of us have it easy. We all choose our hard.

As my relationship with Richard grew, I met Dusty. It was July 4, 2008, the first and only time I didn't have my son with me on his birthday night. Mauriion was with his grandparents. I went to a rave with my friend Lina. Not long after I walked in, I saw the sexiest caramel, mixed man with brown eyes. He was tall, dark and handsome, and he looked like a GQ model. Besides his physique, one thing caught my eye: the beautiful black panther with green eyes tattoo that ran along his shoulder.

We exchanged numbers and began talking regularly after that night.

Dusty would call me every day and every night to make sure I got home safe. No one had ever shown that kind of care for me. I got high just from being in his presence. It was the first time I had felt like I really loved someone. Most of the men I was with only cared about themselves. Dusty was different. He had values and cared about his impact on the world. He wanted to help kids get out of the ghetto. He was direct and he had such a loving presence. Everyone who knew him loved him. He had hundreds of friends, and everyone wanted to be where he was. As we got to know each other, we realized so many divine synchronicities. We felt the same traumatic feelings of neglect, abuse, and abandonment from our parents. We both experienced sexual abuse at a young age. We both had a tattoo with our initials on our left inner ankle that we'd done ourselves at the age of thirteen. All our commonalities made me feel like we were destined for each other. While growing up, we had no money, we barely had enough food most days, and we were both hustlers who took care of our siblings and parents.

One night, we were at his house in the middle of the ghetto. He asked me to be honest with him about what I was doing at the club. I started crying, afraid he would leave me when he learned the truth. Even still, I knew I had to tell him. I opened up to him about the fact that I was the mistress of the strip club owner. Dusty was the first person I could open to about who I really was. Prior to this, I kept my truth to myself. I hid being a stripper from a lot of people, and I let each person know limited information about me and the drugs/activities I partook in. I was as fake as they came, molding my image to each person I connected with. I was ashamed of myself, so there was no way I could tell people what I did on a regular basis. I was sure that if anyone knew the real me, they would hate me. But Dusty stayed. He loved me despite what I did for money.

Being with Dusty wasn't perfect, but it was easy most of the time. He was the first person who listened to my hopes and dreams and talked to me about his dreams for the future. Even though he was a drug dealer, he had this vision of helping teenagers avoid drugs and gangs and all the dangers of the streets. He had gotten into drugs early in life and had experienced a vicious cycle of going in and out of jail, so he wanted to help kids see the pitfalls of that kind of life. He wanted to help uplift urban communities and help people live a more healthy, harmonious life. We started working towards that goal by dreaming of creating a community center to help young people. In the midst of all that dreaming we did, we got engaged and moved into an apartment together. Dusty was the first man who I thought loved me, and I believed what we were building together was actually going to work. He was also the first person I trusted. We decided to save together because I didn't trust myself with money.

When I got into my zone at the strip club, I was making between $1,000 and $4,000 a night. That was the first time in my life I had that kind of money, so I'd spend it like it was nothing. I'd go to Walmart for some trash bags and end up spending $500 on things I didn't need. Dusty was responsible and he told me to start saving money. That was easier said than done. I needed help, so I would give him rolls of cash to save for me. I loved him so much and trusted him more than I trusted myself, so I didn't even ask where he put the money.

About a month after we moved into our first apartment, the unthinkable happened. On May 19th, I was working at the club. Dusty was on his way to pick me up from work and we'd planned to go to a party. He was notorious for being a no-show, so when he hadn't arrived by three o'clock, I just got a ride and figured I'd meet him at the party. After partying it up at the club after hours, I was ready to go home, but Dusty still hadn't shown up. *Where is he?* I thought. *Whatever. It's not the first time he's left me hanging. I'm going home.* Instead, I called his friend and went to Dusty's friend's party with a coworker friend. I assumed Dusty would end up there because one of his best friends had said he was going too. After a few hours, I was partied out and went home. By the time I got home, I was dead tired and went straight to sleep. About an hour later, his sister called.

"Theresa, HE'S DEAD," she said through sobs. As she breathed heavily and cried. "Dusty is dead, girl.

He's dead."

I blinked and then shook my head to unscramble my thoughts. "What the fuck are you talking about?"

"He's dead," she repeated. "They killed my brother."

In that moment, everything stopped. I was in shock, speechless. My whole body felt numb. I couldn't bear the feeling, so I turned to drugs. Whatever was near me, I took it—coke, crack, MDMA, marijuana, pills, whatever. In the days following the shocking news of Dusty's death, I couldn't work, I didn't shower, I didn't eat. Functioning felt useless because my life felt useless. I felt so abandoned and angry.

All I knew was Dusty loved me and made me better than I had ever been. With him gone, I became bitter with God. In such a short time, Dusty and I had built a life together. Our apartment was the first nice, modern place I had ever lived in. We were so thankful to be out of the ghetto, and we had such big dreams of making a beautiful life together. Now, all of that was gone. I hated the sight of our home without Dusty there. I hated life and I just wanted to die. Just when I thought life couldn't get worse, it did.

In the weeks after Dusty's death, all his friends, who had become my friends by default, turned on me. I had moved to Milwaukee just eight months prior to Dusty's death and I didn't really know anyone other than his friends. Somehow, they knew about the money Dusty, and I had been saving and thought that I took the money. What they didn't know is that I had been making a ton of money at the club and giving Dusty nearly everything.

When I walked into a riverwalk Milwaukee bar that was kitty corner from my apartment, I heard techno and figured I would run into someone I knew. Right away I saw Dusty's best friend, Jinx. He looked at me and said, "Man I can't even look at you!"

In shock I cried out, "Why?"

Jinx replied, "We can't find the money that Dusty had. Everyone thinks you took it!"

"What the fuck?" I said. "I didn't steal shit and fuck whoever thinks I did. I didn't give a fuck about that money which is why I didn't know where it was!"

Truth was, even if I did ask where he was stashing the money, who knows if Dusty would have told me. He didn't even tell me his real name. I found out after Dusty died his actual name was completely different than what he told me. As I took two of the biggest emotional losses of my life, I realized that I didn't know anyone and no one around me knew me. I felt like everyone and everything in my life was fake. I ran out of the bar and cursed God. *Why do you hate me? How can you take the only people who love me away? I fucking hate you!*

Dusty was intoxicated and driving, he was with a biker gang doing a large drug deal. There are still many of us that believe he was being chased but we don't know. After Dusty's murder and not being able to find all that money we'd saved, I took a huge financial hit myself. Most of the money that was missing was probably money I had earned. There was no one to support me or be in my corner. My sister was in jail. My brother was in jail. Dusty's sister was there on and off, but she really took his death very hard. At least she knew I did not steal his money, and so did his mom. Yet, they were grieving themselves. With no one to turn to, I felt so alone. I didn't know how I was going to make it. Then, the depression came. I was angry and alone, and I wanted to escape all of the drama and confusion, so I went numb. I doped myself up. In a short time, I had multiple sexual partners because I was straight up desperate to feel any kind of love or tenderness.

In an effort to hide from everyone and everything, I locked myself in my apartment, closed all the curtains, took some pills and hoped for death. I was disgusted with myself and my life. Prior to that, I had asked a friend to watch my son so I could have some time to grieve. That left me free to avoid life and just zone out. All alone, I smoked weed, popped a variety of pills, and drank alcohol during my waking hours. With no appetite, I didn't eat for over a week. I just cried and screamed and cursed until I used up all my energy and fell asleep. When I slept, I had the most awful, violent dreams and I'd wake up completely soaked in sweat.

That's when the entity started showing up and I began having these strange spiritual experiences. At moments when I thought I was alone, I suddenly knew I wasn't because I could feel the presence of something. I'd be in bed and suddenly it felt like something was standing on me. This led me to sober up because I thought I was going crazy. That was the start of me having the darkest experience ever. I was awake and sober for the first time in a long time.

It happened in broad daylight. I was on my bed, holding myself in a fetal position on my knees facing the bed. Suddenly, I felt like I was being choked, but no one was there. I couldn't breathe. The next thing I knew, I was in the darkest dream ever. A shadow creature I could not see ripped my soul out of my body and began dragging my soul up the walls. With a bird's eye view from the ceiling, I could see my body lying on the bed. Then, suddenly, I was thrown into some hellish place with all kinds of demons. They were raping and pulling me apart. I kept trying to escape, but I couldn't. They wouldn't let me go. Finally, I awoke. It was terrifying.

After that nightmare that started while I was awake, I knew I couldn't be home alone anymore. I thought for sure I had lost my mind. I needed help. My friend Ditsy was recently divorced, and she moved in with me. We were both tired of life in Milwaukee, so we decided to escape to Dallas, Texas. For some reason, I thought by leaving Milwaukee I would get away from all my problems. Our plan was to dance in Texas and make a shitload of money. Unfortunately, it did not work out the way we had planned. At the first club we went to scope out, we saw a tall, dark, and handsome man, thugged out drinking champagne. Ditsy and I both looked at each other with the look woman give when they are both single and see a hot dude. That "May the best gal win" look. He stood up and walked past our table. I turned on my charm and asked him his name and invited him to join us. He was a "rapper" called Pretty Boy. He smiled and offered to get us some drinks. We started chatting, had a few laughs, and it was obvious he was all over me. After that was clear, I asked him to show us newcomers around Texas. We were trying to find a club to work at. He turned to Ditsy and said we could go scoop his guy, then they would show us around.

We excitedly agreed.

Pretty Boy introduced Ditsy to Carlos and the two of them hit it off. Carlos was Pretty Boy's gofer, and Carlos did whatever Pretty Boy said. Pretty quickly, Ditsy started acting funny. She started getting short with me, not wanting to work the same shift as me for the first time in four-year friendship. Within a few weeks, Pretty Boy and I started to fall off. I was struggling to make money, and he was pressuring me to widen my offer, essentially to offer sex work. Ditsy's sister agreed to watch Mauriion while I worked, but her offer to babysit was running dry as quickly as my money was. The clubs that were lit wouldn't hire us. I was unhealthy and had a pot belly. Ditsy was super thick in the less ideal places. Compared to Texas women, we had no ass or titties. Ditsy and I both looked like we could have been pregnant. The clubs that would hire us were so slow they were not worth working at. It was a rough time.

By the time three weeks had passed, Pretty Boy had become distant, I didn't feel my son was safe, and Ditsy was acting like she hated me. Her man was disrespecting her son, and that disgusted me. I had such low self-worth that I was willing to "take one for the team" and put up with it all, but even then, I had my limits. As much as I wanted to stay, I knew that if I tried to make it on my own after everything I had lost recently, I would probably end up dead with no one to care for Mauriion. Within just a few months, I flew home, and she stayed. I was back in Milwaukee trying to mask the loneliness I felt.

All the friends I knew when Dusty and I were together had turned on me. They still thought I took the money. But when a new club opened on Brady Street, the truth became obvious to me. Dusty's best friend, who never had any money and never worked, suddenly had the money to open a club on one of the most prestigious party blocks in Milwaukee. He was walking around town like a shot caller, owning a lux restaurant and club. When I saw that, I knew he was the one who took the money, my money. What I learned from that experience is when there is harsh blame coming from someone, they're often the guilty one.

To help cope with all of the loss and betrayal, I did all the drugs I could find. Drugs were being given to me by all kinds of people. All kinds of unknown people were in my home, and I consumed whatever was passed to me without question. It was my rock bottom.

A friend was watching my son so I could grieve, therefore, I didn't have any responsibilities. I was weak physically and mentally. I was so thin my bones were showing through my skin. I was torn between wanting to die and not wanting to leave my son alone in the world. That was the thing that prevented me from actively taking my own life. *Nope, I can't leave Mauriion. He can't care for himself and no one I know will take good care of him.*

I had been in my bed for days, doped up, lying in my own vomit. My friend Melissa and her friend Cliffy came over.

They kicked a bunch of random people out of my house and carried me out of bed. I tried to resist as they picked me up and forced me into the car to go to Melissa's house. Immediately Melissa undressed me and put me in the shower. "This needs to stop," Melissa said. "Something has to give." I realized how much pain I was in and how hopeless I felt. I realized how fucked up I was. I was totally fighting, and I knew something had to change. That's when I finally gave in and started to clean up from all of the drugs.

All of this was happening in my life while I was dealing with another tragedy that affected my mom.

To say my mom lived a hard life is putting it lightly. Her childhood was tough enough, and as an adult there seemed to be one thing after another that pushed her down, stomped on her, and kept her from getting up. Even still, I am grateful that she had me, and I know she did her best to raise me well. What could I expect when she had parents that abandoned her, and no other examples of true love and support is.

Through years of hard living, my mom was diagnosed with cancer in her ovaries and uterus at the age of forty-one. She started treatment right away, but by then the cancer was pretty aggressive. After she had chemotherapy, we thought she was all good. Then, she went through radiation treatment for a short time. It was tough and it took a lot out of her. Soon enough, she decided she was over it. In the final treatment, they realized that the cancer had originated in her colon. She said she couldn't do it anymore. The doctors sent her home with a bunch of medications, but she didn't take any of them the way she was supposed to. Basically, she gave up. She wasn't really improving.

"I'm tired of this shit," she'd say. "I've lived long enough. My life has been hard as fuck, and I'm tired. I'm ready to rest in peace."

I researched the benefits of healthy foods and different types of nutrition treatments for cancer. She refused it all. All she wanted to eat was mayonnaise and cheese sandwiches on white bread warmed up in the microwave. She never considered any of the alternative treatments I or the doctors would suggest. To ease her pain, she began taking pills other people would bring her. I didn't even know what that stuff was, but it caused her to be incoherent to the point that she couldn't even carry on a conversation with anyone.

When she did come to her senses, she would journal. She wrote journals for Letiecia, Joey, and me; just her thoughts about us and her life and how she felt about us. Right before she died, she gave all of the books to me and told me to share the ones she had written for Letiecia and Joey. I read through each of them, and when I finished, I was so upset. The journals she had written to my brother and sister were pages and pages of her thoughts and stories and memories. Each of them took up more than half the journal pages. The book she left for me was just seven pages long.

What the fuck? She must love them more than she loves me.

At the time, I was angry with her. Had I been that terrible as a daughter? All those years when I thought I was the good one, it turns out she didn't even love me. These were my thoughts, fueled by the anger and grief I was feeling watching my mother die. She had given up on life, which made me feel like she had given up on me and my son and everyone else I thought she should care about. Many years later, I realized that my mom could have wrote more in the journals she gave to my brother and sister because she was so afraid of how their lives would turn out that she believed they needed more guidance from her than I did. Even still, it hurt.

Six months after Dusty died, on December 2nd, my mom died. It was her forty-second birthday. I was more angry than sad when she died. In my mind, she had given up on herself and committed suicide. Even as I grieved her death, I was angry with her for giving up on life. Watching my mom suffer the pain of cancer throughout her body and knowing what I knew about the life she lived; I realized that you can't run from your past. You must face it, or else dis-ease will take over in some form. Life lessons that you don't learn from, and traumas you never heal will perpetuate in your children and generations after that. This is not an omen, this is a fact that is known as generational trauma.

You could say it's ironic that I followed the same path my mom did, but it's not ironic; it makes sense. Shame, self-sabotage, and guilt ran my life just as they ran my mom's life. But I knew eventually I had to break the thread and do something more with my life than she'd done with hers. If I didn't, I would end up just like she did.

Mike, my man at the time, came with me to my mom's funeral. I was so drugged up that day, I could barely speak. Despite being on a combination of various uppers and downers, the last thing I said to my mom was, "I promise I will make you proud someday." And I meant it.

After she died, I became afraid of leaving my son. I couldn't stand the thought that he would ever be left in this life without me. The cancer my mom had was hereditary and I had already started having some bleeding in my colon.

I didn't understand why, but my colon would just flare up and bleed at random moments, and it was very painful. It literally felt like I was shitting glass. Because of that, I was afraid that I would get colon cancer and die, leaving my son without a mother or anyone else to love and care for him. I became interested in holistic health and wellness. I started exploring how to be my most healthy, vibrant self. I decided to get sober and that I would do something positive with my life. To me, sober meant no pills or hard drugs. I never considered marijuana a drug. It was a deliberate next step into reclaiming my power, one that proved to be much harder than I ever imagined. But before I could move on, I had to face the darkness that returned to haunt me.

Many days leading up to my mom's death, I would curl up and cry, overcome with sadness. I had lost Dusty and then I'd lost my mom. I clung to Mike out of desperation. It was like a cloud of sadness was hanging over my head. Then, out of nowhere, the entity that had tormented me months earlier returned. It came to me in the night. I would be lying in bed trying to sleep and then something I could not see would get on the bed. The bed would move; I could feel and hear it. It often got on top of me. I would be paralyzed. No words would come out and I could not move. Often, it felt like something was choking me, but I couldn't see a figure or a silhouette. At times, I saw my body lying in the bed as I was being dragged by my throat up a wall. I'd be kicking and squirming trying to get the entity to release me. It wasn't a dream, but more like an out-of-body experience I would watch from the corner of the room. It terrified me each time it happened.

There was no way I could tell any of my friends about this because they would think I was crazy. But I needed answers for why this was happening and how to stop it before I wound up dead. The universe conspired to bring me the answer I needed. In the weeks following one of the most intense experiences with this entity, one thing after another guided me to where I needed to be.

One night, I met a guy at a party. We were all standing around talking, and this guy stopped in the middle of our conversation, looked straight at me, and said, "You need to go to church with me."

The entire group just stared at me. *Where the fuck did that come from?* "Hell no, I'm not going to church," I snapped back. "I believe in God. I'm safe. I don't need to deal with those church folks."

The next day, I went out to eat Chinese food. My fortune cookie said: *Ships are safe in the harbor, but that's not why ships are built.* That stuck with me, and I thought about it for days. Finally, I became fed up with the fear of this creature. I reached out to my grandparents. I never really spoke to them at this point. When I told my grandmother what was happening to me, she said, "That's a demon Theresa. You need to go to church." Immediately, I thought of the guy from the party who had invited me to his church. But to make it even weirder, the next thing she said sealed the deal. "I know a nice church on the other side of town. It's called Safe Harbor." With that, I nearly fell to the floor. *Okay, I'm gonna go there.*

The following Sunday, I showed up in the pews Soul's Harbor Baptist Church in Milwaukee. After the sermon, I asked to speak to the pastor. I told him what was happening. He taught me about the power of the name of Jesus, and he told me to say, "In the name of Jesus I rebuke thee!" I had a tiff with Jesus at the time, so I decided to say, "In

God's name," hoping that would do the trick. In fact, it did. Whenever that entity would come close, I'd find the strength to say, "In God's name, release me!" Miraculously, the thing would stop, and I'd be fine. I felt empowered instantly!

The next time the entity came to me, I was completely paralyzed. I couldn't speak or move or do anything. I had to force the words out and only a whisper was released. That was all that was needed, the small whisper released the entity's power over me--I could speak and move again. I started reading my Bible and then went to sleep. It didn't come back for a while and when it did, I fearlessly rebuked it. As my fear decreased, so did its power over me. That was all the motivation I needed to begin going to church regularly and studying the Bible. Heck, I started sleeping with the Bible in my bed. But the more I studied, the less the Bible made sense to me. I thought it was because I was stupid. *Either I'm ignorant or everyone else is crazy.* Quickly I decided it was my ignorance. With this understanding, I absolutely refused to live a life of ignorance, so I decided to learn everything I could to make a better life for myself and my son.

I was still dating Mike who was a drug dealer, and my intuition started to wonder if he was good for me. Even though Mike was loaded with coke, I felt extremely drawn to him. It may have been the fact that he was a balling drug dealer or that he was cute and rowdy AF, just how I used to like them. Most likely, it was because I was lonely. Either way, a few days later, Mike asked me to be his girl and stop working at the club—I was in. He offered to pay my bills and take care of me. *What a dream come true*, I thought. That was just what I needed at the time, someone to take care of me, because I was exhausted taking care of myself

& everyone else. At this point, my brother, sister, and their significant others all lived off my stripping and hustling money, and I was tired of it.

Mike hung out with squares but had a thugged-out swag about himself. He spoiled me rotten, buying me clothes, shoes, fancy meals, and all the drugs I could snort, smoke, and swallow. He was a sex addict and so was I, so it was perfect. He hardly left my side, so the night demons didn't bother me. Within weeks, I was tired of all of the drugs, so Mike started partying without me. One spring day in 2010, I went to Mike's bathroom and saw a heroin needle. *Fuck this! He may be balling, but I ain't fucking a dude who does heroin.* When I confronted him about it, he denied it, saying the heroin belonged to one of his friends. I knew he was lying.

"Fuck you!" I said. "I'm gone!"

As I walked towards the bedroom door, he grabbed me by the arm. From the strength of his grip, I could tell he was on something, but I didn't know what. I pushed him and said, "Get your junkie ass away from me." He then fell back and almost crashed to the floor. Immediately, he round-house kicked me in the face, and I flew across the room. In that split second, my brother, Joey just happened to enter the room. That's when all hell broke loose. Within the blink of an eye, Mike and Joey were brawling. Mike freaked out and let loose on Joey, punching Joey hard until he lay there balled up in a corner. Joey was on Xanax, so he couldn't fight back. I tried kicking Mike in the dick with all my might, but he just laughed.

"Babe, I didn't mean to kick you," he said calmly as he continued punching Joey.

With a bruised and busted face, I reached down to grab Joey and we both ran out of the apartment as Mike grabbed for me. I knew then that there was no way I was ever going to fuck with him again. That was the best decision ever because within days, Mike had already hooked up with Dusty's sister Kelly and they'd gotten engaged. I was pissed off at Kelly for hooking up with him, and at the same time, I understood. I knew what it was like to be so desperate for attention.

About a week after the fight incident at my apartment, I got a text from Kelly: "This motherfucker molested my daughter. Why the fuck would you introduce me to a child molester?" When I saw that, I dropped my phone. I was pissed and ready to cut Mike's dick off. The calls and texts from Kelly soon turned to apologies and a request to help her. I called Mike's probation officer and Kelly pressed charges. Despite Mike being on probation in two states, he walked free within days of his arrest. Soon after, he found a new girlfriend to do heroin with. I heard that while she was performing oral sex on him, she overdosed at his house. Shortly after that, Mike shot himself in the head. The whole thing was tragic and scared the shit out of me. *Why do I keep attracting these fucked up people who do crazy shit?* I wanted out of that life so badly, but I didn't know where else to turn.

5. MY HEALING JOURNEY

Following those dark days, I embarked on my healing journey, prompted by that spiritual experience with the entity. I began studying religion and questioning the nature of my reality. I began truth-seeking as I realized the devil works in illusion. Anytime we align with illusion, we open ourselves to work with darkness. It opened my eyes to a reality beyond what I could see, and this led me to seek a deeper connection with God. My calling to make a positive impact on the world grew stronger, driven by the losses of my mother and my fiancé. I was determined to make my loved ones proud. This drive to be more wasn't just about me; it was about making the world better for others. I wanted to heal myself and to make my body a place where cancer couldn't grow, so my son would never be left alone. I wanted to make a positive impact and leave a mark on the world that improved the lives of others. I came to realize how much my actions ripple outward and influence those around me. But at that point, I had no idea that I didn't value myself. I still sought meaning externally because I was blinded by a low self-worth I didn't even know existed.

Whether it happens, whether good, bad, or ugly—there is always a gift if you are open to finding it. You just must choose to seek the gift. To find it, you simply have to ask:

I wonder what the gift is in this situation? This child like curiosity works for everyone. God says over and over "Ask and Ye Shall Receive" If you ask, you will get answers revealing the hidden gift. Identifying the gift makes it easier to forgive the situation and appreciate what you gained from the experience. When you pull off the veil, removing the metaphorical blinders, you can stop pointing the finger and realize that you are playing a vital role in whatever you are experiencing. What we blame and criticize for reflects who we are on the inside. We are all human, being compassionate when we react is important. If we are experiencing a lot of hardship, we need to evaluate ourselves deeply. Slowing down during these times is the best policy.

Remembering my humanity while seeking divine guidance is what helps me navigate these challenging times. During these times, I ask God to show me what I need to embrace and what I need to release to create the ease and grace I desire. This mindset takes the preconceived notions out of the equation and allows me to approach life with a childlike wonder. Having an open heart and searching for truth prevents me from defaulting to finger pointing. To embrace this mindset, you must take accountability for your actions and be honest and vulnerable about your role in various situations. A significant portion of my life was spent blaming others, leading to a victim mindset. Shifting from victim to victor changed my perspective dramatically. Now, I reflect on how I contributed to situations and focus on not repeating those patterns. *How did I play into this, and how can I ensure I don't do it again?* Seeing through the crap and believing in truth empowered me to leave Kenosha in search of something better. This conviction that there must be a brighter future allowed me to escape the patterns of my past when others around me stayed stuck in familiar cycles. I dared to believe in a more promising reality. If reality is what we choose to believe, why not choose something better in the future and make it happen?

Even as I wrote this book, I realized that I still felt unworthy of love. This realization was hidden in the shadows deep inside me in a place that I hadn't examined because I didn't realize what true love is. I had been avoiding silence and stillness. This is imperative because God works in our stillness and in our silence. If we avoid these two things, we are asking while not providing the space to receive the guidance and/or healing we are seeking. When my attention wasn't focused on someone else, I was looking for ways to numb my emotions. Wherever your attention goes, your energy goes. Seeking to fix others was a way to feel good about myself temporarily, but it didn't address the root causes of the painful void inside me.

So many of us grapple with addiction, depression, anger, and bitterness because of that thick feeling of heaviness of internal emptiness within us. When I get angry, it feels like my blood is boiling. I used to run to Marijuana when this happened. Now I choose to face it, feel it, and nullify any negativity that comes up. Nullifying negativity is when you deny the power of the negative feeling you are feeling. It is not a spiritual bypass where you are denying your feelings. You are simply denying the power of that feeling over you. For instance, if you think a negative thought such as, "Man I am stupid." Then you nullify it by saying, "Ignorance has no power over me." I would follow that with an affirmative statement such as, "Thank you creator for filling me with your wisdom, strength and patience." These are just examples, feel free to use it and exchange any words you wish to bring in or release. Another way I numbed my emotions was by stimulating myself with a man or woman. By constantly falling in love, I can distract myself from doing the work of silence and stillness. I came to realize the void was caused by a lack of self-love. Working on self-love unveiled the layers of insecurity, which I had to address step by step. Healing isn't a linear process. It's not like you just heal and you're healed. It's like saying to yourself, "Oh, okay, I've learned this and I'm here and this is a level of love. Okay, I love myself." And then you realize now that you love yourself, you must honor your needs, you must speak up for yourself, otherwise you are saying you love yourself and acting like your needs/desires do not matter. There's always a deeper level in healing. It involves gradual growth, learning to honor your needs, and developing ways to ask yourself difficult questions, then face the answers. I highly recommend letting God lead your healing. Expect God to answer you. God wants to speak to you; you must seek and then allow. All throughout the Bible we hear God told Abraham, God told Moses, God told... God wants to support and guide you and it is up to you to make space for that to happen. You only need enough faith to fill a mustard seed. Ask the following questions after taking a few deep breaths. Give yourself a little space and have some paper and a pen to journal. *God, what do you want me to embrace or/and release? God what do you envision for my life? God, what habits or routines will best support my alignment to Divine will, love and truth?*

When you pull off the veil and stop pointing the finger of blame at other people, you begin to realize that you are in control. God will show you where you are out of integrity and what you need to do to fix it. Only then do you give yourself the power and the ability to accurately see what's in front of your face. Seeking divine truth was my way to heal. It involves taking out all your preconceived notions and humbling yourself in a childlike state of wonder. That puts you in a place of open receptivity because if you think you know the answers to the questions you ask, you won't see the true answers, even if they are right in front of you. You must humble yourself and be open, be accountable for your actions, and be authentic about your role in the situation you find yourself in. Then, you have to take action. That's what I did.

GOING TO SCHOOL

The reason I went to school was because I realized that the Bible was not making sense to me, and I just assumed it was because I was ignorant. There was no way I was going to let my ignorance stand in the way of me building a better life for myself and my son, so I decided to go to college.

At first, I tried the University of Wisconsin-Milwaukee. The application process was lengthy, and I hadn't taken any college prep tests, so I didn't think I would qualify. During my first two years of high school, I received straight Fs, but I improved, ended high school with straight A's and graduated with honors. Unfortunately, my transcripts didn't look good, and I feared I wouldn't get in. Sure enough, I did not get accepted, so I tried a new school, Alverno College.

Alverno did not require college prep tests. I applied and was invited to visit the campus right away—this gave me a lot of hope. Initially, I felt very inadequate to even go there. It was a private, all girls Catholic school—I felt so much fear walking into the beautiful campus. During the meet and greet, I took a preliminary exam. A part of me felt extremely ignorant after the test was complete. However,

I was committed to learning and being the best student, I could be. The admissions office told me that all I needed to do was take a few prerequisites over the summer to be admitted in the fall. That seemed easy enough to me. Then, of course, there was the cost. It was one of the most expensive colleges in the area. I received financial aid and still required a grant to cover my registration and books. I didn't even think about how I was going to pay it back. All I focused on was doing it well.

At this time, I didn't know how to use a computer. I also didn't know how to attach a document to an email. But I learned what I needed to know to achieve my goal of getting into college and graduating. The summer of 2010, I was accepted into Alverno College. I was twenty-one years old, the age most college students graduate, and there I was just entering college. I was literally going to a Catholic school and working at a strip club. I was intimidated, but I wasn't going to let it stop me--I was on a mission.

I originally wanted to be a teacher and then build a group home for kids aging out of foster care. I started with all the classes I most enjoyed which translated to history, business, and religious studies. Once I realized I had to master technology to teach, I decided I had to change my major assuming I would fail technology. I hated technology because I was afraid of it. My hands would sweat, and I would nervously itch whenever I was in a tech class. Eventually, an incredible Academic Advisor pointed out that if I changed my major to History, I could graduate on time. Everyone around me thought I was crazy and told me I would never get a job with these courses. However, I knew I wanted to make a difference, and I couldn't do that if I couldn't understand how we, as humankind, got here. I chose a double minor of religion and business. Always passionate about business, I knew I would build an empire one day to fund my group home. Religion was calling my name because of all the experiences I had just gone through—the deaths, the demons, and the rebuking of those demons with a simple phrase.

In religious studies, I learned about meditation (the most important thing we need as humans), and that led me to Jacqui Lane. She was a business coach who was once a stripper. She was beautiful, smart, abundant, and explained that she'd had all these incredible spiritual experiences. To hear her talk about these encounters made me crave those same experiences. The more I researched and talked with her, the more she inspired me. Her YouTube channel helped me learn how she got where she was. She believed that how you start your day sets it up for success or stress. If you start your day with blissipline, you set yourself up for success.

Blissipline, which is the convergence of bliss and discipline, is a practice that begins each day with things that bring joy, or bliss, such as meditation, dance, nature, or/ and gratitude. Vishen Lakin at Mindvalley also teaches this concept. I started practicing it, the results knocked my socks off. Nearly everything in life became easier. I even began writing my course papers in an hour. Slowly and surely, I began meditating, practicing gratitude, and developing healthier boundaries and habits. In no time, I was getting recognized at school and was asked to present in front of the entire school about my spiritual experiences. Fear kept me from accepting that invitation, but I was honored for the recognition. Throughout my entire experience at Alverno, I felt divinely guided and supported.

As I studied history, I quickly realized the commonality of all creations. Everything—every item, product, and transformation—started with someone believing it was possible AND action steps towards that possibility. The book *Transformation and Reaction: America 1921 to 1945* by Glen Jeansonne was especially profound to me. By reading it, I realized everything from the American Revolution to every product, law, governmental office, and civil moment started with a thought, a belief AND inspired action steps towards that new belief. This blew my mind how obvious it was. Learning and then integrating aligned information into my life gave me the real power of transformation. I understood that I could have all of the knowledge in the world, but if I didn't apply it, it would be useless. I was instantly grateful for this revelation. I clearly saw how Alverno's way of teaching, which incorporated core abilities was expanding my consciousness at a marvelous rate.

Alverno's eight core abilities—valuing every aspect of life, decision making, effective citizenship, aesthetic engagement, communication, analysis, developing a global perspective, and social interaction—were embedded into every class. This ensured my personal development, self-discovery, and a solid growth path. It helped me understand that I have power within myself, and that God is the true source of my power. That is what prompted me to search for truth. Studying history and religious studies helped me to understand that everything begins with the belief that something is possible. Then, it takes courage to take action towards making it a reality.

Soon after beginning my blissipline practice, I started experiencing a new reality. I became an opportunity magnet. I received multiple job opportunities from my college. This prestigious school wanted me to tutor for English and be an academic assistant for Organizational Behavior. I would never have expected to be in a position like this because I didn't think I was smart. I didn't think anyone noticed me. That felt magical, until I realized that my professor, who recommended me to be his assistant, was only doing so to coerce me into sex. I felt ashamed and then got pissed off.

This professor asked me to come to his house one night to work on some papers. When I got there, he offered me a scotch, which was my drink of choice at the time. After about half an hour, he said he had a headache, so he needed to take a break from working on papers. We were sitting on his couch in his living room drinking. I offered to leave since he wasn't feeling good. He grabbed my arm and asked me to please stay. Suddenly, it hit me; something didn't feel right. I felt trapped. I didn't want to piss him off by leaving, but I didn't want to stay either. I have no idea how much time passed as I fretted in my head. It couldn't have been more than a few minutes and next thing I know, he forcefully pushed himself on me and began kissing me. Partially in shock, I just let it happen.

After a few moments, I jumped up and said, "I have to leave." I grabbed my things and ran out the door, feeling ashamed. The next day, he called, but I didn't answer.

When I showed up to class as his assistant, I could barely look the other students in the eyes. I felt they knew why I had gotten this job. It wasn't about my intelligence; it was about my body. When that semester was over, so was that job, and I was grateful. In the end, I didn't say anything to anyone about the assault, so no one at Alverno ever knew what happened. They fired that professor for a similar incident with another student, and when I found out, I was relieved and ashamed. I wondered how many women I could have helped if I would have spoken up right away? I'm sure there are other professors at colleges across the country who push themselves on students. I would encourage any person who experiences something like this to speak up, even though I didn't. I know how hard it is, and I know how ashamed I felt. The shame of knowing he was a repeat offender hit me harder than I would have imagined. Being a stripper made it worse because I felt like I deserved it.

That experience may have been the push I needed to get me to stop stripping. Around that same time, I developed a fear of being seen as sexy in business. Because of that, I stopped stripping and went to waitressing. I started to value myself for the first time in my life. I still danced in private rooms, but I felt conflicted inside and always had to be super wasted. Something better was coming, and I wanted to break through everything I had been through so I could be free from the chains of my self-defeating choices.

Thanks to all my college experiences, I started investing in myself. I felt good for the first time in my life, and that's really when my focus on self-care and holistic wellness started. I took religious courses that caused me to research and compare Islam, Judaism, and Christianity, as well as Eastern philosophies and Native American approaches to various plant medicines. This helped me develop my philosophy of Unity Consciousness, my knowing that the divine is in everything and everyone. It also led me to see that there are universal truths embedded within all of the major religions. I also realized that each has its own gifts, and it is up to us to seek truth and release anything that isn't truth without judgment. Just like us humans, each religion has truth and deceit. We need to develop the gifts of discernment to know when we hear the truth. When we focus on aligning with Divine truth, love and will, we are guided to be the best versions of ourselves naturally. This means we develop unconditional love for ourselves and all that is.

There is a difference between loving yourself and practicing self-love. Because you can love yourself on a conscious level and not love yourself on an unconscious level. To love yourself on an unconscious level, you have to retrain the subconscious mind, which takes repetition. We all have a level of love, but if we don't practice it daily, we are not honoring, valuing, trusting, and loving ourselves. For instance, many people love plants and then don't water them, they don't feed them, and the plant eventually withers and dies. This is the kind of superficial love that doesn't dig deep and nurture. I had a concept of love within that wasn't deep enough to actually take actions to ensure that I was giving my mind, body, and soul what it deserved and needed to thrive. This is one of the reasons I love Alverno because they required me to dig deep into my mind to understand what I valued and why. They didn't settle for any superficial answers. I had to explain everything I did in every class.

To this day I value Alverno College for everything I learned there and for the growth they led me through. They are a pass or fail school, so either you totally understand all concepts while displaying their abilities to a specified level, or you don't pass. There are zero multiple choice questions. Instead, most of the tests involve teaching others what we learned while effectively working in respectful balanced groups. If someone didn't pull their weight, the rest of the class had to help them get on board by encouraging and helping them. Doing their work for them would lead to failure.

Their teaching approach is practical and comprehensive. No matter what class you took, you had to display the skills of valuing, decision making, problem solving, analysis, aesthetic engagements (engages in informed artistic and interpretive choices), and civility. For example, in one of my math classes I had to take notes of how I spent my time for at least a week and then talk about how my values influence the use of my time. This was an in-depth assignment, so trying to get away with something like: "Oh, I value my family," or "I really value life," just wouldn't cut it. What does that mean? How does that show up in your actions? They weren't going to take any surface-level responses. I had to dig deep and fully explain my response and show how it showed up in my life. That assignment showed me that I was spending two hours a day getting ready, putting makeup on my face, and straightening my hair. Then I calculated how many hours that was each week (14 hours) and each month (56 hours). Over a year's time, it was an average of 224 hours... I compared that to what I was doing for my physical fitness, for my nutrition, and other activities. That exercise made me realize how superficial I was.

I saw clearly that I was guided by subconscious programming, not being conscious of what I was doing, moving out of habits not awareness. And so, the more awareness I gained, the more action I took to create new habits that were beneficial for all of me. Everything from my daily routine to what I eat, to how I responded or reacted in any situation, to the thoughts in my mind, the little voice that never really goes away, all of that is part of who I am. When I began to focus on who I am, I went from judging everyone and everything to appreciating and loving everyone and everything.

We once did an activity where we had to calculate how many times, we judged someone or ourselves. Until this assignment, I thought I was a kind person, that was a lie. I realized I had been judging everyone all the time, including myself. You simply cannot be a kind person while walking around judging and criticizing people all the time. If I saw someone walk into a store, I would judge what they were wearing. I would judge their size, their facial expressions, how they walk and talk. I'd judge the couples I saw together whether they looked like they were both on the same level of attraction. Looking back, I did this because inside of me I was using older men, and I assumed the worst of me in everyone I saw. I would automatically make this judgment without even thinking about it. When I took inventory, I was like, *Holy crap! I'm judgmental AND I need to change.*

Judgements weigh your heart down and make you feel more disconnected from Source. Until you begin to dive into forgiveness work, you don't even realize how heavy your judgements are. Every time you judge someone externally; it comes from a judgment you have within about yourself. I didn't want to vibrate negativity; I wanted to vibrate positivity.

After that class experiment, I chose to turn away from sin and stop judging others and myself. I choose to have faith that my life would get better if I took the necessary action steps. Beliefs dictate your courage and trust, which determine how quickly you heal. Even Jesus, after performing a miracle, told the sick who had been healed to not go back to the same people because they wouldn't believe in the miracle of their healing, which might cause the sickness to come back. That caused me to ask myself, "Who is around me? How are they living, are they honest? Do they strive to improve their lives? How are they adding to my life or depleting?" All those energies from every person I hung out with, whether conscious or unconscious, influenced my vibration, which influenced what I was focusing on.

To avoid overwhelm, I continued with school, and I stopped going to church. I kept doing my blissipline, reading scripture and journaling. For the first time in my life, I had proof of my hope. *Everything I was learning proved to me that anyone could be anything they desired as long as they worked for it*. I was motivated and determined to make this world a brighter place. Everything I was learning fueled me with more belief and more motivation. Alverno's courses built on each other in a way that was super synchronistic and profound. I started seeing synchronicities everywhere. The constant evaluation allowed me to see where I was out of alignment with my words and actions. This was important to me because even though I vowed not to judge others, I still had a strong belief that this world was a cruel hard place to live. Before I had Mauriion, I said I would never have kids because I was afraid to bring a kid into this world because I thought it was all going to end. "We're all going to blow each other up," I would say. But as I continued my studies, I learned that reality is what you make it. I can choose to see the world as a dark scary place, or I can believe it is a good loving place. Our external world will always show evidence of what we believe... We create our own reality.

In the beginning, our truth is shaped by our environments, but it is our duty to explore and find a deeper truth. All the world started together, and God gave everyone pieces of information because God loves everyone equally. Therefore, God wouldn't just give one all the information. It is up to us to research, seek, and find truth, to put together the things that are aligned. As I explored the concept of alignment, I deepened my meditation and self-care practices. So much of my studies took me deep within, which helped me see things outside of me from a whole different perspective.

During my last year at Alverno College, I got an internship at the Center for Teaching Entrepreneurship. That's where I met the late Redonda Rogers, the Chief Executive Officer. She was the first person I opened up to about my story. I told her all about my troubles as a kid, and that I was a stripper with a couple of sugar daddies. Seeing all of me, she loved me and believed in me. She was such an inspiration. I never felt so seen and accepted by anyone. She taught me how to network and to become the change I wanted to see in the world. The mission of the center was to help kids in poverty start their own businesses. We targeted kids who were getting in trouble for dealing drugs. Funny thing is, that behavior showed their entrepreneurial skills, but those skills were used in a depleting way. Our environment showed them a healthier way to use their skills.

The volunteer work I did there helped me have an impact on those kids and I started loving my life. It is hard to be sad, depressed or angry when you see that the actions you are taking are making the world a brighter place. I knew for sure that the best for me was yet to come!

6. A FRESH START

Once I graduated from college, I went through an interesting phase. I started partying and didn't stop for months. One day, my niece and sister were at my apartment. I started singing my favorite song of the time, "Turn Down for What?" by Lil Jon. My niece, at nine-years old, started crying, saying, "Can you stop? You've been turned up for too long." That is when I realized that it had been two months of madness and I decided to stop, settle down, and get a job.

After applying for several jobs and receiving no responses, I went back to work at the strip club and asked Richard for some advice on what to do. He connected me with his niece Mary, who owned a recruitment agency specifically for the auto industry. She got me an interview with the president of a car dealership. At the interview, I told the guy my big dreams. I wanted to eventually start a group home for kids aging out of foster care to help them develop both foundational life skills and self-care skills so they could be empowered when they turn eighteen. It didn't feel strange to tell him all of this in an interview. I had learned the power of voicing my intentions, and this seemed like the perfect time to express the dreams in my heart.

Afterwards, Mary called me and asked, "What is wrong with you? Why did you tell him all of your dreams and ambitions? Girl, he wants someone that will be there long term, not someone who just wants a temporary job until they find something better. Next time someone asks you what goals you have; just say you want to work for a company you can grow with!"

As it turned out, sharing my big goals made me lose that opportunity. It was Thursday, date night for Richard and me. Really it was always Richard, me, and 5-11 of his male friends. At dinner, Richard turned to me and said, "What the fuck is wrong with you? Why did you blow that job? You think the president of a successful auto dealer wants to hire a broad who thinks she can save the world? They don't! They want someone that will shut the fuck up and get shit done! You fucking blew it. That would have been an easy job. You embarrassed Mary. Don't fucking do it again!

My face turned red. I was so pissed that I slammed a triple shot of Crown Royal, then went outside to smoke some weed. I was beyond embarrassed, yet I was too scared to do or say anything back to Richard. While I loved him, I needed him at this time. I knew I had to be careful what I said to him because pissing him off would only make things worse.

Soon after, Mary helped me get an interview for a business development position at a Toyota dealership. During that interview, I acted as if I had no dreams or big goals. Apparently, that's what they wanted, and I was hired on the spot. Despite having a credit score of 500, I bought a Prius and started my career. During training, I was blown away with my manager named Lavette. She was in her twenties, a powerful, beautiful black woman with a voluptuous figure and a great wardrobe. During my first week, she showed me the system, which was very basic. People would call, email, or chat and we would get them quotes and schedule an appointment. But getting an appointment right away wasn't easy.

Lavette didn't believe in follow up. She had been in the industry for years and said that if they don't schedule right away, they are probably just browsing. For some reason, to me, that seemed like I was leaving money on the table. So, I waited for her to go to lunch and started following up on old leads. My first month, I outperformed her in appointments booked. Of course, after that, things started to get tense between us. In the second month, I was an appointment-setting queen, and nearly all of the appointments began selling. By then, Lavette was very angry and getting meaner and meaner by the day.

Competition can make people do some crazy things. Even though I never saw Lavette as my competition, apparently, she saw me as hers. All the deals I was making caused her to be upset. One day, we were both in the hallway outside of the office and she started screaming at me. I don't even remember what she said, but she acted like she was ready to fight. I couldn't believe it. As soon as the guys heard the commotion, the whole dealership ran upstairs and got between us. I quickly ran into my office because all I wanted to do at that time was work and get paid. I didn't show up there to fight her or anyone else. Honestly, I was scared of her.

The next day, Lavette was fired because of that incident, and I became the manager. I was asked to recruit someone to help in the business development department, so I hired my best friend at the time, Tasha. She and I worked at the strip club together. She was funny, beautiful, positive and a walking party, my kind of friend. I showed her the ropes, and we worked and played hard for weeks on end. We even drank while working almost every day. With a little liquid courage,

I could reel anyone into the dealership. The sales team was always coming into our office and the owner started every day and ended every day in our office, typically complimenting me in a slightly flirtatious way. I felt so powerful all because of a little consistent attention.

Cliff, the general manager, was a sweet guy in his sixties, with kind eyes. While he was always very kind, he was never flirtatious and that made me respect and trust him. One day, he said we needed to talk about the pay scale. "Theresa, I'm very proud of the work you're doing," he said. "In fact, the owner told me to alter your pay scale to make your appointment bonus higher than your sales bonus." I was floored. With that adjustment, I could make more money because I would have more control over setting appointments. The way I saw it, this change to the new pay scale was a raise and I accepted it. At the end of the month, I did the math. It showed that this new system was actually a demotion. I made about a thousand dollars less with this new system. When I told Carl, he apologized, saying the change had come from the owner himself.

I went into the owner's office, and I told him that I was making way less with this new pay scale. He said, "You are good, but if you expect to make over $60,000 out of college, you're crazy and you're replaceable." His response pissed me off to my core.

My throat choked up and I held back my tears, then took a deep breath and said, "Ok, goodbye." Fighting back the tears, I then went into my office with my face clenched up and asked Tasha if she wanted to go to lunch.

On the way to the pool hall, I told her what had happened, and she was just as pissed as I was. While waiting for our food, I got on the phone with Mary and asked her to help me get another job. She had just received a message from Umansky Motors that they needed a Business Development Manager right away, so I agreed to go check it out. Together, Tasha and I both decided to not go back to Toyota. We had a drink and then I called Pete (my first sugar daddy) and told him I wanted to go shopping for some professional clothes because Umansky Motors sold four high-end brands:

Mercedes, BMW, Porsche, and Volkswagen.

Later that day, I did some grounding and prayed that Umansky would want me. Not wanting to waste any time, I decided to go over to Umansky Motors that same day. With my sexy, yet professional black Calvin Klein dress highlighted in gold, makeup, lashes, and heels, I walked into the dealership looking more confident than I felt. I watched heads turn as I went into the assistant store manager's office. He seemed nice and slightly preoccupied. When I told him about my sales experience, he wanted me to start immediately, but there was a catch; I had to pass a drug and background test first.

At that time, I was still smoking weed and doing cocaine seldomly. On Cinco De Mayo—I partied hard so I was terrified, but I knew I would find a way to pass the test. My brother had place he would get pee when he was on parole and had to do frequent drug testing. When I called to tell him I needed the hook-up, he told me where to go. I went to this store that had a back room where they kept the pee, bought a small rectangular plastic container filled with an unknown yellow substance. To keep it warm, I hid the bottle inside my bra between my boobs. I didn't know if the testing facility had some way to monitor people while they left their urine sample, so I prayed that God would help me pass the drug test. A couple of days later, I had an offer with a base pay nearly twice the amount I was getting from the Toyota dealership! I was so thankful and felt like I was a big deal.

Looking back, I realize that I'm a natural at business development, but I didn't realize it back then. My boss, Mr. Magic Mark became one of my favorite people. He was tall, with an athletic build, fair skinned, with a glorious white goatee, and very handsome. He believed in me from the start, even when I didn't believe in myself. His confidence in me helped me gain confidence in myself, and he always had my back. One time, I mistook his generosity and kindness for a possible interest in me. I was always attracted to the boss, so, of course, I hit on him. I asked him if I could join him for dinner. He laughed at me and said, "No. You're a kid, for God's sake. What would people think?" At the time, I hated him for saying that and laughing in my face because I thought he rejected me due to my looks. Now, I understand it wasn't my appearance; it was my age.

When I was in the business development center at Umansky Motors, I was young, sexy, and right out of college. Many of the salespeople had been there for decades. I came in and instantly developed a system before I knew what a system was. I learned very quickly from my work at Toyota that the riches were in the follow up. Naturally, I treated people how I wanted to be treated, and I developed a follow-up method that was consistent, but left some space for the buyer to think about the offer.

At that time, the salespeople in the business development center were told to call three times a day. I only called three times a week, but I varied when I called and only left a voicemail after trying a few times. I also sent emails every other day so that no one felt bombarded. I knew that business development is a numbers game, so when I arrived at the office, I was focused on making a hundred or more calls per day. As soon as I started getting low on energy, I would go outside to ground and recenter myself so I could get back at it. The tone of your voice sets the stage for how the information you share is received, so my vibrancy always came through over the phone. My seemingly scattered mind served me so well in this field because I easily jumped from person to person, kind of like I did during my childhood.

Despite all of my success, I still didn't have confidence in myself. However, years after I left Umansky Motors and applied for work with the government, Mr. Magic wrote a letter of recommendation for me that knocked my socks off and let me know how good I was at my job and how much he respected my work. He essentially said I played a pivotal role in taking a failing dealership to number one in the area in just three months. That meant the world to me.

The entire time I worked at Umansky Motors, I continued working at the club on the weekends. I was waitressing, technically, but still couldn't turn down money in the VIP rooms. When I went out with Richard on Thursday evenings, he would call it "boys night" to keep his wife from joining or getting suspicious. For me, it was a date night with my lover and his friends. Occasionally I would get my friends to join us, but most of my girls were from the club and they were afraid of Richard, so they didn't want to hang out too much. He had a lot of rules. We couldn't be on our phones, no outsiders could engage with us unless they knew Richard, and if they knew Richard, then they kept their space from us.

While I worked at Umansky, I would pray that my coworkers would not see me out with Richard. I was at a point where I was embarrassed to be seen as a sugar baby, but I was addicted to him and wildly unstable. I wanted to believe that I was a woman of substance, yet standing next to a married man made me feel worthless. Even with Richard paying my rent and me making a good salary plus weekend tips, I was living paycheck to paycheck. Our age difference was obvious when we went out, so I assumed that everyone knew I was a sugar baby. Richard was very attentive, which, in the beginning, was nice. I had never felt so loved. In the end, though, I began to get annoyed with him pawing over me—I felt like he owned me, like I was a toy he picked up and put back on the shelf whenever he pleased. The shame and guilt overtook the feelings of love.

It was 2017 and I was living in a beautiful four bedroom, 3,000-square-foot home with a closet bigger than the room I grew up in, located right off a highway in Greendale, Wisconsin. I had a huge yard and a river in the back with a park next door. I was living my American Dream with a brand-new Mercedes in my driveway—in my name. I couldn't believe it. I was happy with my things and yet miserable with my life because I was addicted to making money. I worked non-stop and even had the customer resource management system on my phone for 24/7 access. As soon as someone sent an inquiry—it didn't matter if it was 7:00 a.m. or 10:00 p.m. I responded right away. This is how I helped Umansky go from a failing dealership to number one in the region in just a few short months. Throughout my entire life, I always worked hard. I intensely pursued anything I set my mind to. I had no idea what I was doing to myself.

Soon, tensions in my home rose to unimaginable heights. My brother, Joey, came to live with me when he got out of jail, shortly after Dusty died. Joey and I were fighting on a regular basis about one thing or another. To help him get back on his feet, Richard loaned him $10,000 to start a food truck. Sadly, Joey didn't follow through on his plan to get that business going. Instead, he changed his mind and decided to build his own food truck. Within a month, the materials he purchased with Richard's money—really, just a bunch of junk he'd picked up here and there—just sat there in the driveway, and he hadn't made any progress. The neighbors started complaining to the city and eventually all of Joey's junk was towed away. It was a total waste. Richard was pissed, Joey was full of remorse and guilt, and the combination of it all caused tensions, defensiveness, and depression between the two of them.

Of course, all of that just brought more stress into my life. The more stressed and depressed I became, the more problems I had with my colon. When the swelling and bleeding began, I didn't know what to do. It felt like I was shitting glass. Just sitting hurt, and I feared the worst. When my mother died from colon cancer, her half-sister Angie started calling and we connected deeply. Angie introduced me to some really cool people on YouTube, like Ask Angels, some lady who was instantly healed of cancer in her neck, and Abraham Hicks, an inspirational speaker and channeler. These people helped me start believing in possibilities and believing in myself. Angie offered to help with Mauriion and take Joey off my hands. With that, I flew out to Colorado Springs and spent a couple of weeks. I knew right away I wanted to move there, so I gave Umansky Motors my notice and off we went to Colorado for a fresh start within a month.

Leaving Wisconsin wasn't easy, and getting set up in Colorado cost a lot of money. I had to pay my rent a few months in advance in order to get the lease since I didn't have a job. That took most of the cash I had, which wasn't much because while working at Umansky, I spent money as quickly as I made it. When I arrived at the apartment complex, I was so angry I started crying. Being in such a hurry to move, I had leased the apartment sight unseen, and the complex looked nothing like the pictures. Reminding me of my pitiful dating life. The pictures showed a luxurious condo-like setting, but what I pulled into looked like a huge run-down, fixed-income complex. The paint was old, and the buildings had paper-thin walls. But I was stuck with it because I had signed the lease.

I found a job right away, but it was in Denver, more than an hour's drive from my apartment in Colorado Springs. The recruiter promised a salary of $65,000 a year, which was better than anything I could find in Colorado Springs. It was a job selling business phone lines for T-Mobile door-to-door, street-team style. The people I worked with were amazing; however, they demanded long hours and two weekly team-building events. All of that was tiring and time consuming. They also lied about my pay.

They told me I would start making money right away. My weekly salary during training was supposed to be $500. It turned out that the pay was $500 once the training was complete. And all the sales I made during training went to the trainer. The trainer then decided when each of the sales reps were ready, and that's when we got the $500. After three months of not receiving a paycheck and being so broke I couldn't buy food, the owner's boyfriend took me grocery shopping out of pity. Afterwards, I started to wonder why I was putting up with this. I wondered if they would ever promote me and why I was willing to work twelve-hour shifts and drive for three hours a day for free.

With no income, and in need of food for me and my kid, I quit and got on welfare. Every day, I prayed for something to give so I wouldn't end up homeless. During that year, I went through ten jobs, each with one dramatic ending after another. Mostly I was the victim and had no idea that my victim mentality created those horrible experiences. But once I finally realized that everything, I was experiencing was a result of my beingness, everything changed.

7. GETTING INTO BEAST MODE

You can play the victim role like I did for years and keep experiencing crazy or dissatisfying events. You could sit there and blame other people or decide that the way you were brought up is the reason you don't have the life you want. It's easy to point the finger at other people as the cause of your life being fucked up when you're out of alignment. But when you get straight with divine truth, you step into alignment. That's when you start to experience your own truth, your own power. That's when you come to accept the fact that no matter who or where you are, whatever you are going through, you are the cause. And because you are the cause, you have a choice. Whatever is happening *to* you is actually happening *for* you.

That's when you get into Beast Mode. This is the space where you just get things done and nothing in the world can stop you. To rise up in Beast Mode, you need the right mindsets.

These are the mindsets I choose over and over that help me get into Beast Mode:

- Adaptability, Versatility
- Resiliency
- Fast Learner

- Fearlessness, Flexibility
- Thirst for Truth, Knowledge, and Power
- Plant Medicine

ADAPTABILITY, VERSATILITY

People pleasers tend to be super adaptable. We naturally adapt to whomever we are trying to please. In the strip club, this was fun at first. I came up with all kinds of stories when entertaining clients. The stories I told depended on the audience. This was my first experience learning marketing without even knowing what marketing was. I could play the victim, the schoolgirl or the whore. I found joy in every character I chose once I had a few shots or party favors to juice me up. I think it was more about the attention. When I was flying high and feeling amazing, I made a ton of money and usually had fun. When I was depleted, angry, or not making money, I hated every aspect of it. I think most of us have a similar story. When things are going well it is easy to be happy. True self-mastery is when we can be happy no matter what is happening externally. This sounds easy but what do you do when your kid is having medical challenges, and you see him skirting the possibility of death?

I literally had to go through these experiences many times. When I was 16 and they told me my son might not make it past the week. I affirmed God's power and victory over death, and it worked. I had faith because I refused to lose hope. However, my son had 3 near death experiences in 2024. I panicked for the first two. The last one, I choose to trust God and when the fear and overwhelm was too much, I went into nature and started running or hiked until I felt better. He survived and I was able to be a healing presence by his bedside instead of a worried, fearful presence. Sure, that meant taking time for myself, allowing myself to rest when needed and pushing through the pain when my body called for release. The key to escaping the overwhelm is surrender, stillness, physical fitness and compassion for yourself in whatever capacity brings you the most peace.

RESILIENCY

I've been resilient my whole life. It is one of the most necessary skills to have in today's world. At the same time, it is always messy, and the process is typically full of fear because bouncing back from a painful situation is hard. I moved to Colorado because, even though I had this prestigious title, an incredible career as a Business Development Manager at Umansky Motors, I was still addicted to the club. Every weekend I would go there to party and waitress. Essentially, I was getting paid to party. I would make $1,000 to $2,000 a night. I found it interesting that when I didn't need money, it came easily.

I loved making money even if I didn't spend it on myself. The idea of moving to Colorado forced me to save about $15,000. Within a few months of saving that cash, we moved. However, in a very short time, I fell on my face. Over and over and over again, everything I tried failed. I couldn't even get hired for Uber. Finally, I got hired for Lyft, but I couldn't make money even though I was working my tail off. I had a dozen jobs in one year, some that didn't pay me, others where I was threatened. It was unbelievable. Everywhere I went, I failed.

Now I know that I created it because I didn't have any value for myself. I didn't feel worthy. I was scared to go crawling back to the club where I depended on men, but I was desperate and running out of money. So, I went to my old tricks; I tried to get a strip club job. Dancing in Colorado with the altitude was extremely hard. After one song, I could barely breathe. They didn't hire me. They told me I was too fat. I was hurt, but eventually, I found a shitty, hole-in-the-wall club that would accept my body. So, I stripped there and did Lyft on the side. I lasted three shifts at that club before my body gave out. I just couldn't do it.

At one point, Celeste, my best friend, came to my rescue from Wisconsin. By the time she arrived, I was at the end of my rope; I literally could not afford to put gas in my car. I didn't have money to feed my son. As I sat there in tears, Celeste said, something so simple: "What about your affirmations? Go do some affirmations or something."

My immediate reaction was to say, "Fuck affirmations. They're not working." And I just continued crying.

She laughed because she didn't believe in affirmations at the time. Then offered to take me grocery shopping. I was very prideful and used to paying for everyone and everything in my life; well, except for the sugar daddies. So, I swallowed my pride and accepted Celeste's offer. By then, I had become very focused on my health and was into a holistic, organic, whole food, vegan diet. As we walked up and down the grocery store aisles, I cried like a two-year-old because I couldn't afford the foods I was used to eating.

"Theresa, I know you want the organic beans," she said. "Go ahead and get the organic stuff you want."

Through tears and a snotty nose, I cried, "I can't afford organic." It was a sad scene.

I am so thankful Celeste came to my rescue. The beautiful ending to this is that a few months later, I started my company. A year later, Celeste was struggling with work, and I was able to employ her. Being able to give her a job when she needed it was the most rewarding thing ever, and quite frankly, I needed her because I needed employees. It was a win/win solution. With consistent reflection we can see the divine synchronicities that tend to bring people and events full circle. So many times, throughout my life people that were under my management or managing me reversed roles. This further deepened the importance of treating everyone how I wanted to be treated. The Universe is a beautiful friendly place, when we embrace beauty and friendliness within. This sounds easier than it is to practice. It is easy to be nice to nice people. Often, we interact with people that are disrespectful and/or condescending. If I am feeling good honoring, valuing and trusting myself, it is easy to be kind to a difficult person. When I am low, I can feel my blood boil in the face of disrespect, and I want to unleash my inner wrath. This is when it is most imperative to rise above because the only reason, we feel low is because we are cutting ourselves off from Source. When we are full of light, we are full of truth, love, and compassionate understanding for those that are suffering.

FAST LEARNER

The reason I learn fast is because I dive deep. This is both beneficial and can be a hindrance. It is beneficial if you are learning about one thing from multiple angels. It becomes a hindrance when you try to learn multiple things from multiple angels. If you are changing too much at a time, it is hard on the body and the body, mind or soul can feel unloved and/or unworthy. Unconditional love means that we love ourselves completely as we are. That means we need to be easy with ourselves in the realm of change.

A desire to change typically arises from a perceived problem. I have noticed every time I think I have a problem; it is an indication that I am not living my truth in some form. I choose to see all problems as an opportunity to get closer to God. Naturally, I go straight to prayer for direction. Affirmative prayer has been my secret sauce. I absolutely love the prayer flow I learned from the book, "Discover Your Divinity: A Modern Guide to Affirmative Prayer" by Linda Martella-Whitsett and Deeann Weir Morency. It helped me understand and feel comfortable with prayer. I deeply encourage you to read this book as my brief description cannot give this divine work of art the justice it deserves. The book guides readers to pray within the framework of 5 movements:

1. I open to a new Possibility-We must be open to receive a new awareness, understanding etc.
2. I recognize God is-they recommend using the 12 powers i.e. faith, strength, wisdom, love, imagination, understanding, will, order, zeal, power, release, and life etc.
3. Integrate an I am statement tied to the powers
4. Affirm what you realize, what you have or/and what you know
5. Appreciate whatever feels most aligned at that moment

Here is a prayer example for embodying divinity:

I open to the infinite allness of Yahweh (original name of God/Eternal Source). Yahweh is the epitome of grace. I am one with the grace of God. I see the beauty of God in all that is. In this awareness, I realize I can move through life with ease. I know that Divine Grace is active within me now. I honor this grace within and extend it to those around me. I give thanks for the graceful expansion of my consciousness. And so it is.

When we pray, we are in direct communion with Source. This is why I love praying! When things are hard, I ask God to guide me to the right people, places and information that will best help me see the challenge the way God sees it—as an opportunity for my growth and expansion. If fear is involved, I denounce the power of fear over me. I am not bypassing fear; I am affirming the fact that fear has no power over me. Feeling fear is normal, we have a choice as to whether we allow it to take control of our mind, body, and soul.

I trust the prayer as it is stated and complete. However, I like to, I look for spiritual leaders that I align with, I get a book or two on the subject and I look for documentaries from organizations I respect. I also look for podcasts that align with information related to my challenge. This way, I am reading, watching and listening to information that will help me form my own opinion on how to rise above the perceived challenge.

THIRST FOR TRUTH, KNOWLEDGE, AND POWER

My goal is to reach my maximum potential, it took me years of studying, researching, and getting certified in a variety of modalities before I did what was needed to achieve this. All along I had no idea the answers to my questions were simpler than I imagined.

My maximum potential is achieved by focusing and allowing the embodiment of the Holy Spirit to be the source of my everything, including my inspired actions. By setting the daily intention to be a clear vessel for Divine will, love, and truth, we begin to receive the guidance and support needed to clear our vessel. The support provided from Source is a direct reflection of the focus, intentions, and discipline we have. I have daily mind, body and soul practices that I do consistently. Yes, I am human and have skipped and/ or fallen off at times. Each time I do, I see my internal and external environment move from order to chaos. The funny thing is, when I fully committed to being a clear vessel, my world turned inside out. My identity shifted dramatically with relationships, in my career, and with my habits. All of this completely disrupted and aligned to what I had dreamed of and more.

This reorganization is uncomfortable and messy, but it is also the most epic adventure of a lifetime. I couldn't fathom where I was going while everything around me became completely unstable, like the floor was being pulled from beneath me. Every time it happened, my life dramatically improved. I held on to that belief which developed my ability to trust that whatever is happening is happening for me.

The lowest points are where my deepest trust and faith developed.

I now realize that we live in a world of distraction. As it turned out, I had the most dramatic distractions you can imagine. Because of that, I was so hyper-focused on the drama that all my power went there. I allowed everything to pull me away from doing what was needed for me to rise above the drama. I needed deep silence and faith. Even God said, "Be still and know that I am God." God is always simple and compassionate. Simple is kind. The ego is often complex and difficult to please. My ego had me on all kinds of "spiritual missions" to keep me away from truth—to keep me distracted from going within.

FEARLESSNESS, FLEXIBILITY

I learned that the best action is divinely inspired action. Most of the time, if the Holy Spirit is guiding you to do something, it is going to be new. Maybe you are being guided to foster a kid, start a business, or pursue ministry even though you judge churches and could never see yourself in one.

Expansion and adventure require courage and a willingness to change some things to welcome new things. There are going to be times when the only information you have to act on is a little intuitive nudge to do something. Often, the nudges make no sense, yet it is in those nudges that the entire universe is supporting you beyond your wildest dreams. You must trust in your divinity to fulfill the dreams you are blessed with. Not all of them will pan out. Some of them may simply serve as hope bubbles to keep you in the grateful mode of receiving and allowing the Divine to do its work through you. This requires deep trust.

The image that gets me through these tougher times is the one of me floating in the middle of the ocean, being fully supported by the Divine, knowing sharks and all kinds of unknown predators are beneath me, and trusting that I am safe because we are all one. God created the cosmos. God is in the shark, God is under the rock, God is in your heart, God is in my heart. God is in all His/Her creation!

8. EMPLOYEE TO ENTREPRENEUR

My first year in Colorado Springs was painful. I rented a "luxury apartment" online without seeing the property in person—when I pulled into the parking lot, all I could do was cry. Looking around, I realized I had moved from an upscale home to what looked like the projects. I wiped my tears and started unpacking anyway. I had great credit but no job. Most landlords didn't want to rent to me, so I felt a need to suck it up since I had already paid six months in advance.

As soon as I unpacked, I started looking for a job. I had no idea what I wanted to do so I began networking to get to know the area. Getting a job there was gruesome. I submitted hundreds of applications. Some places called back, most didn't. I started applying for everything, just to increase my odds. Visionless, passionless, and scared out of my mind, I took entry-level positions from anyone that would hire me.

Unsurprisingly, one after another, each job ended in some epic drama.

I started to believe that even though one job didn't work out, the next one would be better. After failing forward that first year, I began to lose hope and belief in myself. After a couple of months of being broke and nearly becoming homeless, I committed to a morning routine to help me feel better. This was the third time I had made a strong commitment to feel good. The last two times, everything I tried went to shit until I felt better internally, then my external world lit up slowly but surely, beyond my wildest imagination.

To raise my vibration, I started my morning with a walk in nature. Then, I would do a form of energy medicine with either Donna Eden or Qi Gong with Lee Holden on YouTube. As I got ready for my day, I would listen to Power Thoughts Affirmations, also on YouTube. Then, I would meditate and/or write out my gratitude. It sounds like a lot, but when incorporated into my day, my morning routine cost me roughly forty minutes extra. At the same time, the morning routine charged me up and made me feel like a manifesting queen. Everything I wanted I was getting. Heck, I boldly stood up in front of my bestie Reana Clarke and her mother and declared I was ready for a tall, dark, sexy, disciplined, loving, supportive, vegan man who earned at least six figures. One week later, I met James. He checked every single box, even the shallow ones.

A few weeks later, I had multiple job offers. I took a position as a job coach. For the first time in my life, I felt like I was doing something positive. I was terrified at the idea of helping others find employment, but it felt good to do good, and the company agreed to work with my son's school schedule. The job was offered to me despite me applying for another role. The universe spoke, and I was desperate. I fell in love with the job immediately. Within a couple of weeks, I was promoted to Director of Supported Employment.

At the time of my promotion, James and I were a couple months into dating. He was a safety officer in the military and was deployed in Germany, but I didn't care. I had dated many men in prison; at least he was gone for work. Everything was awesome. I was flying so high I didn't care that I was making a few cents over minimum wage. I placed more people in jobs in my first month than that company had placed in five years. My Supported Employment Department began blowing up with new clients. Consequently, we had to hire more staff to keep up with the demand. I loved being a part of the hiring process even though I had no training, and I sucked at making initial judgments of people. I love everyone and naturally overlook people's flaws with an open heart—not a good trait for hiring.

Carrie was our first hire. She was a short overweight mother of two who came from a call center background. She had no experience or qualifications, other than mandatory trainings and the high school diploma required for the position. She was so nice at first, and we became friends right away, but her true colors began to show. When we moved offices and she was put in the main room with the other entry-level employees, she started to yell, scream, and act like a child whenever things didn't go her way or when I gave her an assignment to complete. Carrie soon became tight with another employee named Tracy. They would team up and act like children, disagreeing with anything I said and being inappropriate and unprofessional. Within a very short time, their behavior became almost unbearable. I knew it was a toxic environment, but I loved the clients and didn't want to leave.

Right before Christmas came the final straw. Tracy had already paid me less than all the other department heads. She was kind to them and cold to me. She bought all the department heads these small gifts, but she didn't have one for me. I was crushed. I had been left out my whole life, so this was another incident that made me feel less important or valued than everyone else. The final straw came when she bought everyone's kids presents for Christmas except mine. I could not work for someone who would be that cruel. With the environment completely out of alignment for me, I knew I had to leave. I just never would have thought that starting a business would be the next step in my career.

Brittany was a vocational rehabilitation counselor for the State of Colorado. She matched companies with qualified employees and oversaw companies like mine to ensure the clients' needs were met and that the bills got paid. We worked together a lot. She even called me her number one provider. When I left my job, I asked Brittany for a reference because I wanted to stay in the field.

"Of course, I'll help you," she said. "You're the best provider I've worked with in years. In fact, I think you should start your own agency."

Hearing her say that really messed me up because I didn't feel I was qualified, but her encouragement boosted my confidence and made me believe I could do it. She insisted I was qualified as I had direct experience and had the educational requirements already, then she directed me to the application to work with the Division of Vocational Rehabilitation (DVR). Even though I thought she was crazy, I called James to tell him what she said. He told me to go for it. Seeing James as the most logical person I knew, I figured if he thought I should go for it, I should. Thinking of a name was a struggle, but I decided that this was my time to own all of me, so I went with Rubi's LLC; Rubi being my middle name. I offered Employment Services where I helped individuals with disabilities gain and maintain employment.

When I started my business, James was my biggest supporter. He told me how to get the business incorporated and create bylaws and I completed the DVR application myself. Even with all that set up, I still didn't feel like a business owner, but I was excited at the chance to help individuals with disabilities increase their opportunities to get employment. Within days of getting approved, I got my first client placed with a company. He had been waiting more than two years to find work and had not even had an interview. Within a month, I had multiple clients placed and had to stop taking clients because I was running ragged. Through it all, I worked on my lack of confidence, worth, and value so I could see myself as the entrepreneur I am. My confidence developed significantly as I helped my clients find their strength, voice, and value. Even though I was terrified, I kept going. Regardless of all the successes, I couldn't see it as my success. It is hard to see what you don't believe in, no matter how obvious it is.

Despite my success at matching employees with other companies, I was terrified of hiring employees for my own business. Knowing my natural willingness to trust people —even when they don't deserve it—made me fearful that I would hire the wrong person, someone who would ruin the reputation of my company or steal money from me or unfairly treat those we were helping to find jobs. Because of that, I vowed to avoid hiring for a couple of years; however, life had other plans.

After being involved in a severe car accident, I was forced to hire employees. With my spine in constant pain, there was no way I could run the business and do all the work myself. Failing my clients was not an option, so I called my bestie Reanna and asked her if she knew anyone looking for work. She connected me to a guy we had met on a previous worksite who was perfect. I hired him while in bed recovering and did my best to train him on the fly.

My first year, I operated out of a shared office suite inside my condo complex. It was all good until one night I decided to have a party. The huge condo complex had a lot of amenities, including a recreational room and gym, which is where I held my party. I wanted to dress up and feel sexy that night, so I put on a booby-licious blue and white jumpsuit that had cut-outs on each side. It was soft and sexy, my favorite combination. I was intoxicated, drinking my favorite gin and ginger, and went to refill my cocktail upstairs. Walking out of the recreational room and onto the elevator, I saw a client and an employee, and they saw me. I was so embarrassed and ashamed that I was drinking and my boobs on display. I couldn't speak, I just waved and turned away. The client—a tall man near my age with dark curly hair—came over to say hello. He was bashful and kind. I apologized for my attire and practically ran away. I worried about it the rest of the night, feeling like I was unprofessional for being in my sexiness. I didn't realize at the time, but hiding my body was one of the ways I dulled my light. I was afraid that if people saw me as sexy, I would not be considered intelligent or professional. It is amazing how limiting beliefs creep in behind the scenes. I didn't even know this was a limiting belief at the time.

After everything I'd been through in my life, I had become aware of my tendency to overthink and second-guess myself. My evening ritual was always a rush of self-sabotage. At the end of each day, I would mentally review my day for all the stupid things I had done or said. I am not sure when this started, but I do know that it went on for years. Even with all this immense self-sabotage, I was still empowering others and growing tremendously.

It doesn't matter how messed up you think you are. God is always in charge and God is in everything: the good, the perceived bad, and the ugly. This is why sharing your story is so important. The more you reflect on the lessons you learn, the more you can appreciate how much you have grown. It's inevitable for other people to see how you've grown through things. Just like when you lose or gain some weight, everyone tends to see it before you do. Most people notice without saying anything. But what's most important is for you to notice, no matter how long it takes.

People I grew up with have messaged me on Facebook to say how I inspired them to believe they could get out of a problem or make a change in their life. Many of my friends have gotten off hard drugs and out of abusive relationships triggered by beliefs cultivated by seeing me get through things. If they hadn't sent those messages, I would have never known the impact my life has had on them. Even still, it's hard to believe because I know I'm still a work in progress. We all influence everyone we are connected to, even if we're not trying. It is truly remarkable how much we influence others without even knowing it.

9. GROW THROUGH WHAT YOU GO THROUGH

"You don't make mistakes. Mistakes make you."

Whether the growth is vertical or simply the replacing of existing cells, some form of inner growth is inevitable until death. We grow whether we want to or not. Your choices determine whether you flourish or not. Why wouldn't you choose to nourish your mind, body, and soul to flourish? I feel the only reason to flourish is to lift others up as we do, kind of how the natural world shares excess resources in a forest.

If only we could be more like trees. Anytime we see a deficiency within ourselves or our environment, we tend to see it as a personal problem. Anytime we are angry, judgmental, or shaming and blaming ourselves or others, we are operating from ego, better known as dis-ease. Any dis-ease or dense emotion is a sign of belief in separation from Source. Love is gentle, kind, supportive, compassionate, and empathetic.

Often, we get mad at ourselves over things that don't turn out the way we expected. When this happens, we often look for the mistakes we can perceive. Looking back to the natural order of things to reflect on the spiral of life that is present in every being is important. You have to own the steps you took to get there to avoid the same experience in the future. This is a requirement for success. Blaming, shaming, and whining throughout the process is a choice too. If God creates in spirals, who are we to question a self-perceived back step? When we are disappointed in what we see, it is because we are not seeing with our God-Mind.

While writing this book, I went through a very hard life phase. After blowing up in the business world, having opened my spiritual gifts, things began to crumble. I will write about that journey in the next book, but for now, just know that it was a wild ride. In short, after dedicating my life to God, I started to confuse God with my ego's voice. Following the ego leads to death, pain, and sickness. Within the span of a year, my son nearly died three times, I had multiple points of pure psychosis, and more rebirths and identity crises than I can count. I went from being a miracle magnet to being a force of pure chaos and destruction. I was like a baby learning to walk, falling multiple times each day. Eventually, I nearly died, so I quit everything, then went back to the basics, developing my relationship with God.

I had been looking outwardly for God's favor instead of tuning into the unconditional love my heart was designed to be. I studied for hours in search of truths and a state of being-ness that could only be brought to the surface from my direct intention and actions leading towards my own unraveling. In the midst of it, I got caught up in false realities, matrix programing, or what some might call a series of familial, physical, mental, and emotional crises. During it, I choose to play into fear and believe that this world was an unfriendly place. I also developed the belief that God was punishing me.

Now, on the other side of that dark and painful time, I can hardly believe that I am thanking God for that homework assignment. While taking the Foundations in Unity Course by Unity Church, I thanked God often. The midterm was to develop my own Spiritual Development Plan. I knew the three areas to address would be mind, body, and soul. The first few weeks went by, and then on the last three days, a significant shift happened. That final week, I declared that I was done struggling, and it was time to thrive. The next day, my residual income 10-xed! The biggest pain I was experiencing was financial and that literally shifted overnight!

Prior to this, all my finances had dried up. I had over $200,000 in commissions earned and so many people who owed me money, but hardly any money came in. I went from earning upwards of $100,000 a month to bringing in only $1,000 a month. At the same time, I had developed an insane amount of debt. I truly believe that all my fear and resentment clogged my income from flowing through to me. While in a coaching group with eight women, the Coach took us through a belief exercise related to our money blockages. She guided us through a "finding money" exercise where we had to identify our limiting beliefs and fears around money, going all the way back to our childhood. It was so powerful. Sure enough, a week later, I found $1,000 in commissions that were underpaid. I wasn't the only one in the group who got results. In fact, everyone in the group found a decent amount of money. The coach did exactly what I am doing now, she planted a belief, and our faith brought it about. Your life can be changed in an instant. The more you believe in this, the more you will achieve it.

Where does the belief come from? Beliefs come from your choices, whether conscious or unconscious. You may ask, "How can I choose what is in my unconscious mind?" You may not feel that you contributed to the beliefs that are in your mind because you were raised by parents who taught you how to see the world around you. You learned how to engage with the world by whomever raised you. What we often forget until the mid-life crises hits, is to seek out who we want to be once we become adults. We all think we are choosing who we are but if we don't consciously examine our beliefs, we truly have no idea what beliefs we are operating from. God will only relieve you of weaknesses that you are aware of. Your brain will only let you perceive what it feels you are ready to perceive. In order to accurately perceive truth outwardly, you must come from a place of coherence. You must know how your mind, body, and soul best operate to be aligned with your highest potential. Divine intervention is the intrinsic and outer evidence that makes us question our current reality.

CHOICE AN UNDERVALUED SUPERPOWER

Choice is one of your superpowers that you, like most people, have forgotten you have. It is your free will, the very foundation of your being. Every choice is rooted in what your subconscious mind believes to be true. When the pain is too much, you can choose to surrender to your Higher Power, which I refer to as Source. God, Allah, or any name you prefer to use can easily replace Source.

Every choice you make is either a choice based on fear or love. We all have both light and darkness within. We are all either always emitting fear or love vibrations to the world and cosmos. For the most part, utterly unconscious, we are all either Warriors of Light or Warriors of Darkness at every moment. When you are vibrating love, being grateful, or in service with a pure heart, you are a Warrior of Light. You are radiating frequencies of love to everyone and everything you encounter. When you are in this state, you emit a psycho-physiological coherent frequency that alters your emotional and bodily functions. You feel energized and optimistic, almost like you can feel your cells tingle or dance as they vibrate with so much high energy.

When you are a Warrior of Darkness, you are angry, worried, depressed, stagnant, judgmental, or simply apathetic. You choose your state every second of every day consciously or unconsciously by where you decide to focus your attention. Seeing beauty in all things is a choice and finding joy in change is a choice. Making the same decision over and over again is also a choice. The deciding factor for most of us boils down to whether we think we can make a difference in this world or not. In fact, we are always emitting the frequencies that shape the very structure of it.

If you want a loving, peaceful world, you must create a loving, peaceful internal environment. It starts with choosing to be a Warrior of Light. My way is only an example. Your way is the best way to bring out your unique "lightfullness". You are loved and supported by many unseen beings, who are ready to help you 24/7 as much as you desire their support and are open to receiving their guidance. It is in embracing your unique vibration that you will discover the hidden gifts within.

The wounds of the world allow the light in. When something painful happens, you can choose to change or be bitter. When my sister decided to kill herself at the age of 35, I lost my mind for a bit. When she did this, I was still in a state of understanding how all the events in life fit together. When I separated myself from the drama and the pain of her death, I chose to improve my mental health so that I was not ready to kill myself for any external events. I had a lot of suicidal thoughts after she left. I had all kinds of demons feeding my pain. The pain from those wounds served as motivation to become mentally strong.

The same thing happened when my mom died, I chose to make her and Dusty, proud by going to school. I decided to make the most positive impact possible by becoming the best version of myself. You can choose to allow any pain to be crippling or to be healing. Either way, you will feel the pain of your choices and your actions when you resist or ignore the light God is leading you into. In the same way, you will feel the joy and the peace of God's loving light when you accept that every experience in life is leading you to evolve as a Warrior of Light.

I felt the pain most of my life and still, when I talk about it, I feel it a little bit, only now it's not overwhelming. I see the power that pain created within me. I am now in a place where I am completely unstoppable. Anything I desire, I am going after it. I'm nearly fearless. I'm becoming more and more fearless by the minute because what do I have to be afraid of at this point? I've already been through hell and watched myself grow tremendously from the experiences and people that hurt me the most. I turned all my pain into power and will continue to do so for the rest of my life.

I am calling on you to release any people, places, or things that no longer serve your highest good. Know that anything God removes from your life is for a higher purpose. If the love of your life is toxic and you are called to end the relationship, trust that God will bring you back what he has taken in the most beautifully majestic way.

Change is typically the hardest part of meeting your warrior within. If we look at nature, we see that change is gradual. Physical growth of all beings—human, animal, and plant—is all done gradually. For instance, a baby starts with an egg and a sperm, in other words, an idea (egg) and action (sperm). Science confirms that with consistent nourishment (kindness, gentleness, love, light, etc.) that seed grows bit by bit until it dies. We see the same thing when gardening. We plant the seed, nurture it and allow it to grow slowly into whatever beautiful creation it is designed to be. Back to habit building and micro-shifting. The best way to build a habit is to visualize it seven or more times and celebrate each time. Micro-shifting creates lasting habits.

If your goal is to meditate for one hour daily, slowly build up to it but start small and slowly expand. A few minutes a day with minimal increases is highly suggested. Approach your goal in realistic, bite-size chunks, rather than trying to jump in on day one for a one-hour meditation session. That won't work. Do it in short sessions until your time increases daily. Observe your progress over the first 28 days. First, consistency is the focus, this will also help you build trust in yourself. The more you trust the universe and yourself, the more fun your journey will be. When you declare your worthiness for abundance in every area of life, things will begin to shift naturally. The more you resist change, the deeper you suffer during the ascension process. Suffering is a part of life, and you choose how long and much you will suffer.

TECHNIQUES TO IMPROVE

My way is just an example. Your way is the best way to bring out your unique "lightfullness." What brings you joy? That is what brings about your light. If dancing, art, games, sports, hiking, camping literally whatever lit you up as a kid, that is what you need to do to bring about your light.

With a charged inner light, you can easily receive the guidance from God directly on what steps to take in life. Regular rest is required so that you stay charged and can integrate the light codes coming in. Light codes are bits of information that heal and empower you to hold more light within. Think of it as a spiritual upgrade. They are coming consistently from multiple sources, including this book. The sun, the moon, and all forms of life have various forms of light codes embedded within. We integrate these light codes with rest and stillness. The more you rest in silence, the more you hear your unique vibration tune. By embracing your unique vibration, you will discover the hidden gifts within. God loves us all equally and gives every single one of us countless opportunities to embrace the unity within. Stepping into unity means to be one with all that is— your inner and outer realm. To be one within means to love, accept, and honor all aspects of yourself, especially the dark stuff that you want to hide, even from yourself.

We all start off with lots of darkness. Darkness cannot exist in the light, this is why hiding darkness gives it power. Bringing darkness to the light transforms it into light. The wounds of the world allow the light in; therefore, the pain from these wounds serves as the catalyst that creates Warriors. You can choose to allow the pain to be crippling, or you can choose to allow the pain to transform in to power.

I'm not saying I don't feel the pain. I felt the pain most of my life and still, when I talk about it, I feel it a little bit, but it's not overwhelming. I now see the power that it created within me. I am now in a place where I am completely unstoppable. Anything I desire, I am going after it. I am fearless—even when I feel scared as long as I push through the fear. After all I have been through, what do I have to be afraid of at this point? I have already been through hell and watched myself grow tremendously from the things that hurt me the most. I turned all my pain into power and will continue to do so for the rest of my life. I consistently choose to be a victor instead of a victim.

How you perceive truth depends on what you choose to feed your mind, body, and soul. We all have light and darkness within us. You are feeding each aspect of yourself either light, darkness, or if you're anything like me both. What are you giving your attention to? Are you giving your attention to the pain and the labels, or are you choosing to believe in something more? If you truly believe in something more, you're willing to try anything to get out of that pain. If you choose to believe that God is in you and that you are a child of God, then nothing can stop you. Back that choice up with daily connection and intention to be a vessel for Divine will and you too will be unstoppable in your own way.

The techniques that I provide here are all free and only take a few minutes. I am not asking you to meditate for an hour—even though I hope you build on your practice as you see fit. To create change, you must start with simple, short techniques and build your way up as you are comfortably guided to whatever practice and length best serves you. Find a way to have fun with this and it will be fun. Forcing yourself to any extreme regiments will only lead to resentment. Start small and build. You always have a choice.

Even with all the tools that I have, I can still get caught up with stressing or worrying at times. But I choose to feel it for a few minutes or a day, whatever time frame feels appropriate for the situation. You can turn your day around at any moment by making the very decision to do so. Feeling crappy? Find a funny movie, go for a walk, do something you absolutely love, shake your body, or do qi gong or some kind of energy medicine or breathwork. Any improvement or shift in energy celebrated is perpetuated. Even giving yourself a high-five, a self-hug, or a compliment can shift your energy and train your brain to look for more things to celebrate. Be your own experiment. Do a self-care technique and tune in and scan your body from head to toe in search of energetic improvements. With time, you will notice which techniques benefit you most in particular situations.

This simple check-in helped me to establish a baseline so I could see and feel the difference that the techniques made. I started noticing all the external and internal challenges that popped up when I didn't follow my self-care routine. Even this was beneficial because every time I fell off my routine, I felt the effects and was motivated to recommit. That commitment allowed me to build a deep discipline that validated how effective the tools were for me. When you start a new self-care routine know that it is ok to flounder. Don't beat yourself up over this; it is normal. Instead, tune in, notice how you feel when you are in your routine and when you're off. Soon, you will have so much motivation to keep doing your routine that you won't have to think about it. The best way to raise awareness of your progress is to keep a journal that indicates how you feel and what you did for the day. Your feelings are the messengers that guide your inner compass.

The best way to raise awareness of your progress is to keep a journal that simply states how you feel and what you did for the day. Note what went well, what you are grateful for, and what came up that you can improve in the future. Keep track of any divine inspiration. Is there an animal or insect that keeps appearing to you? Is there a color or type of flower you keep seeing? These all could be signs of what is unfolding. The more you look for divine synchronicities, the more you will find them. The more you see the signs in front of you, the more you will believe you are on the best track for your success and development. Play with this, make this practice your own. To help support you on your journey, I made a guided breathwork video called Embody Heaven on Earth Now. To access this free resource, visit https:// rpempowerment.com/warrior-of-light/

Me at my office embodying my light

PAST AND PRESENT SITUATIONS AS A TEACHER

Is there ever a point when you're done doing the work? I personally believe that we are all here to evolve. This means learning and growth are inevitable. At the same time, you can choose to learn from a place of being in a state of love or fear. If you are learning from a place of fear, learning will probably be painful. If you are learning from a place of love, it will be less painful. Some lessons resurface until you are absolutely done with them. Once you know in your mind this will not affect you again, it has no power over you.

I declared I was done with unworthiness in 2022. I decided I was worthy of my values, of getting paid, that I was worthy of true love, and that I was worthy of all of my desires. When I did, the world began to show me the imbalances in my life while rewarding me dramatically. My agency soared financially and my health and personal life plummeted. Imbalances are a sign of weakness. God wants you to neither run towards anything or from anything. Instead, we are meant to be in balance, to walk the narrow path wholly satisfied and grateful for all that we are and all that we have.

Once you know something is off, you have a choice to continue with this imbalance in your life and relationships, or to declare something different and better. It could be a friendship or a work environment. Usually, it's everything. If you have an imbalance in one place, you have it everywhere. I have hated the quote, "How you do anything is how you do everything" from the moment I heard it because I was living a lie, and that statement pointed to wounds I wasn't ready to face. The thing is this quote is so true.

Choose how quickly you ascend by taking the necessary steps to declare that you are creating boundaries that honor yourself. You are learning to trust yourself and those intuitive guidelines that are constantly presented. The guidance that comes when you decide you want to be a vessel for Divine love, will, and truth is usually the exact opposite of what you thought you wanted. Therefore, you have to surrender and release judgements and fears by standing in your power to fully honor, trust, and love yourself.

I made 2022 my year of worthiness, and I started paying myself $500 a month. Within three months, everything in my life changed. I had a breakup with a long-term partner of five years. This was the healthiest and most stable relationship I had ever experienced, but there was no passion. I realized that I require a healthy amount of passion and deep intimacy—mentally, spiritually, and physically—for any romantic relationship to work for me. We tried our best and eventually he gave up. Simultaneously, I found out about the parasites, and so much more, and then I got the opportunity to be a referral partner for the Employee Retention Credit (ERC). This was huge, my agency made nearly a million dollars from this opportunity while bringing billions of dollars to the business community around the nation.

Around that same time, a friend taught me a simple technique of connecting with God. Before I met her, I thought most people were lying when they said they talked to God; either that, or something was wrong with me. It didn't make any sense. I had prayed for years and never heard anything back, or so I had thought. When she told me how easy this technique was, I did it instantly. I was afraid that God might not talk to me, but I did it anyway! She told me to pray and ask to be a vessel for divine will, love, and truth. I did it and immediately felt the most loving lightful connection that brought me to my knees in joy filled tears. This simple practice, done with a pure heart, will do wonders for anyone. I have expanded on it to help with creating more ease and grace for the integration process. At times, you will be guided to modify practices based on your highest calling as well. Play with this. Follow your heart, as the more fun and joy you bring to it, the more fun and joy you will experience.

The expanded practice is as follows. Once I became super serious about embodying Divine Presence, I did this hourly or more if called for seven days. The repetition is purely for you—you need to believe you are a vessel for Divine will, love, and truth. First, choose a color to represent Divine Light. The color that produces that best feeling will always serve you best. Once you have your color/s you are ready for the process.

1. The process is simple, imagine a color or a rainbow (any color you prefer).
2. Next imagine a funnel, a tornado, or a pillar of light in that same color coming down directly from Source.
3. Imagine that light permeating every cell in your body.
4. Thank God for continuously deepening Its presence within you.
5. Thank your cells for continuously making room for more Divine Presence to fill.
6. End with dedicating your life, work, everything you think, do, say, and be to Divine Presence. "I dedicate my life, my work, everything I think, say, wear, do, be, experience, and encounter over to my Divine Creator."

It's that simple. To me, this technique is a life hack. The truth is whether or not you choose to embody divine presence, divine presence is in you. You are loved and perfect as you are. The presence practice is simply for us to remember the divine presence within. The more we focus on the holy, the more holiness we will see in our life.

As you keep seeking, you will eventually see one small sparkle of light, then another and another. Ultimately, you will cease to resist, and you will accept your pathway, your journey, the love of Source, and your place in this world. You will embrace the Warrior of Light that you are.

Having survived what I've been through, I felt to my core I was a Warrior of Light, only to be brought to my knees during a 2-year whirlwind of facing every fear I ever had. I faced every form of abuse and was nearly bankrupt. I spun my wheels trying to control the situation that was out of my control. I realized early in 2025, it was time to drop my armor and completely reinvent myself to adjust to the new Earth. My warrior mentality was outdated, and the new upgrade was so unclear....

ABOUT THE AUTHOR

Theresa Rubi Garcia is an award-winning entrepreneur, and transformational guide who helps individuals awaken their divine potential through holistic wellness, energy work, and her signature LIGHT Coaching™. A survivor who has turned adversity into wisdom, she empowers others to release limitations, heal deeply, and step into a life aligned with joy, truth, and purpose.

A single mother and first-generation college graduate, she cared for her son with severe disabilities for over two decades, managing all aspects of his care while building her business. Her ability to lead through adversity, including a personal caregiving crisis in 2023, has defined her resilience and inspired her mission to help others rise.

Theresa's leadership has been honored globally with the **CXO 2.0 Conference Business Leadership Excellence Award**, the **Fluxx Award 2025 for Social Impact Architect of the Year - Health & Wellness, USA**, and multiple recognitions from Appreciation Financial, including **Top Recruiter of the Year (2022), Top Cash Flow Earner (2023), and Diamond Earner (2023)** — celebrating her impact, influence, and commitment to elevating others. Theresa is currently working on her next book, *Bound by Duty, Broken by Abuse: The Plight of an American Caregiver*, which sheds light on the unseen sacrifices, atrocities and strength required for being a family caregiver in America.

When she's not teaching her signature HOTT Technique or speaking on *How to Become a Miracle Magnet*, Theresa serves as a prayer chaplain, platform assistant, and retreat leader at Unity Spiritual Center in the Rockies, volunteers with Finding Our Voices, and is completing her Ph.D. in Bible Interpretation through the International Metaphysical Ministry. A true nature lover and resilience in motion, she is also a dedicated trail runner, conquering the Rocky Mountains every chance she gets.